BeThat Mom

10% of all proceeds from the sale of this book are donated to charities dedicated to supporting girls and women around the world.

BeThat Mom

Ignite Your Passions, Organize Your Life
& Embrace Your Family!

TINA O'CONNOR

Cataloguing Data available from Library and Archives Canada

Text photographs by Tina O'Connor, unless otherwise specified in the text
Cover and text design by Tania Craan
Cover photograph by Gerry Wilson Studio/CA
Author photograph by Melanie Molloy/In Tune Images

Published in Canada by Be That Books™
www.bethatbooks.com

ISBN 10: 0-9879154-3-6
ISBN 13: 978-0-9879154-3-6

Printed and bound in Canada

This book is dedicated to my Mom, Janet Legere.

I am who I am because of you, and I now have a complete under-standing of what I put you through all those years. Thank you for caring about me, for being open and honest with me always, and for the support you still give me every day.

You are always positive and smiling, always looking on the bright side. Your daily dose of "Morning Motivation" (the-morning-motivator.com) continues to inspire me. Our five years of "Wicked Women Wednesday Lunches" together is proof that if you choose to make something important in your life, the Universe will help make it happen — no matter what!

Moms like you make the world go 'round.

Tina

Contents

If you want to 'Be That Mom', you'll need to eat and cook like her! Feeding your family right is a big responsibility, and if you want it to be fun and low-stress, it will require planning. Keep it simple. Kick those boxed foods to the curb and embrace whole foods into your life to keep energy levels up and illness away!

Maintaining your family's health "naturally" starts with a good night's sleep for everyone! Learn how to start your own "Natural Medicine Cabinet" to cure what ails you and your family.

Pave the way to an organized home by clearing the clutter out of your life! This chapter details an action plan to make a de-cluttered home a reality.

Using the principles of Feng Shui, any home can be turned into an organized palace. Find the key to success and fulfillment in the rest of your life using this Chinese method in every room!

Tips and suggestions on affordable ways you and your family can have FUN together. Whether it is for a day at the zoo, a camping trip or a Mexican beach adventure... Family Fun is key to building strong relationships.

Foreword

"Start as you mean to go on."
– Tracy Hogg, the Baby Whisperer

The above quote conveys a truth I learned when I first became a Mom. It is a truth we all know; however, we often forget and find ourselves scurrying through life. Admittedly, I too find myself in this situation sometimes — but, we get through the day with no casualties and begin each day as though it may be different.

Then, I met Tina. Interestingly, it was our children who brought us together. I am not the type to normally read or seek out self-help books (though I do require help!), so I can honestly say I likely would not have come across her book at all.

But... as I read through ''Be That Girl'', I found myself starting to believe. I also might have found myself agreeing with a lot of it, and recognizing that I had more in me than I remembered — Motherhood will strip away ones identity away at the speed of light! It wasn't just Tina's words that struck home, it was the way her narrative played like a good friend sitting in the room with you, guiding you and encouraging you to get it done better. She makes it sound easy, but completely puts you through the paces. What do you want from life? What would you change?

"Be That Mom" is Tina's second book of inspiration, packaged up to help you be the kind of mom you have always dreamt you'd be! As moms, we are often the last to take care of ourselves and there just never seems to be enough hours in the day for us. Everyone NEEDS us!

Sitting down and working through her exercises was not only important, it was extremely helpful! When it is all written down before your eyes, the goal is much easier to see. Tina teaches us how we really can 'Planet Do It' and be the best girl - woman - Mom that we can be!

Thank you Tina for reminding me that I need to make the time to get organized and de-cluttered. I always feel like the time will just magically fall into my lap; however, the reality is I need to set the time aside and JUST DO IT! I am the ultimate creator of my journey and I owe it to my family to make it as joyful and as fun as it can be.

Join Tina on your own journey to "Be That Mom"! You'll be so happy you did.

Samantha L. Nickerson

Introduction

"It's all in what you believe!
If you think you can, you can...so think you can!"
– Janet Legere

Be That Mom. Calm. Relaxed. Happy. Amazing. Enjoying life with your children. That's the way it should be and that's the way it can be. You just have to believe it.

You may be pregnant with your first child, have teenagers at home, or be enjoying your empty nest. This book is for you. If you are reading this, it is likely because you are a mom (or you will be very soon), and once a mom, always a mom — even if there are times along the way when you feel you might like to change that!

Whether you are a new mom, older mom, full-time mom, step-mom, or single mom... this book is for you. No matter what your title, the role of "Mom" is the same: to love, inspire and guide another person through their life and provide opportunities for them to learn to take care of themselves. But there are many challenges along the way.

We are constantly fighting against messages that are telling us we are inferior and that we need to give our kids more material possessions for them to be happy. When this is combined with the pressures of creating opportunities for our children, it can create a lot of stress in our lives.

As moms, we have a lot going on. We have to keep our homes clean and stay on top of the laundry so it doesn't pile up. We have meals to cook (and clean up after) and gardens and yards to tend. We have to get our children to and from school, make them lunches, drive them to their lessons and sports team practices. We have to arrange and drive to play dates and plan birthday parties. And if that isn't enough, some of us have full-time jobs to go to — every day!

Then there are yoga classes, coffee dates with friends, reading a good book — all the things we do in those precious little bits of "me time" that are so few and far between. As Moms, we stretch ourselves incredibly tight, but just like a rubber band, over time that tight elastic will wear down and then... SNAP!

But it doesn't have to be like that. Life can be joyful, fun and lighthearted instead of harried, stressful and heavy. We can all choose to have it that way.

Since my family uses the more colloquial term "Mom" when referring to the family matriarch, I was curious to see what the dictionary had to say about it. However, when I typed "Mom" into Merriam-Webster.com, all it provided was a link to the definition of "Mother." Other than "a female parent," my favorite definition, of the word "Mother" was this one:

> something that is an **extreme** or **ultimate** example of its kind
> especially in terms of scale. the mother of all construction projects

Mothers, then, are a very special breed of talented people who are the "ultimate" of their kind — regardless of shape or size. Moms are exposed to **extreme** situations and they become the **ultimate** in giving, and receiving (with a focus on giving)!

Being a Mother (or Mom) is not something you are born into, it is something you must *become*. How do you "become" a Mom? Well, first you'll have to start with some hanky panky...

Becoming "That Mom," however, isn't quite that easy. It's something that requires determination and desire. Who is "That Mom" in your mind? What is your ideal life situation? I'm here to tell you that if you want it, you can have it. Period. The secret is knowing what you want as a Mom and a person, and understanding why you want it. Desire to be the Mom that you want to be... laughing through every moment, loving yourself and being an amazing mentor to the little people you are molding into full-grown people, the ones you are shaping and with whom you share your time. It's up to you to go for it!

The moment the doctor confirms that you are, in fact, pregnant, or the moment you see the positive marker appear on your drugstore pregnancy test, or the moment you sign the legal papers that commit you to being an adoptive parent your life will change forever. You will find yourself smiling as you think about all of the wonderful things a child will bring into your life.

But then that smile will fade as you begin to worry about all sorts of things, like what you might have been eating or drinking during that time when you still didn't know you were pregnant, or whether your finances are going to be sufficient to support an addition to the family, or whether or not you'll be able to handle your current employment duties as your belly expands? From the moment you understand you are going to be a mom you will begin to think way too much about *everything*. You'll be overcome with guilt and worry right from the start.

When I was pregnant with my first daughter, Trinity, I remember so clearly the elation I felt knowing that my body housed a tiny living "peanut" that was growing into a beautiful baby. But I also remember all the worrying! Since you can't see what's happening inside you, how are you supposed to know that everything is OK? I realized that you've just got to have faith. Faith that your body will do exactly what it is supposed to do. There's really no other way around it.

Preparing for that first child was intense. The focus was on the pregnancy and the childbirth process, learning all about how to make it through nine months of renting your body out to a tiny tenant and then pushing that tenant (which has now expanded considerably) out of an impossibly tiny door.

But that's just the beginning of things. What about the next 30 years? They don't teach that in your birthing classes. Surely these skills are innate, natural, passed on from our parents, and will just come to us whenever we need them. Right? Yeah, right. I can tell you that nothing prepared me for the shock of suddenly becoming a mother. All the planning and preparation that my husband and I did suddenly seemed useless when we looked into Trinity's beautiful eyes.

Thankfully, I had my own Mom around to guide me. I was also an avid reader of parenting books and I had a group of likeminded new mom friends that I had met in a Moms101 class for brand new moms. Those first months were definitely not easy. I would often hole myself up inside the house with Trinity and stay there for long periods of time. I found it difficult to even get a shower in or feed myself. My new-mom friends organized weekly trips to the Zoo, forcing me to shower and get my butt in gear. It helped me tremendously. Even though it's not an easy thing to do, getting out of the house and interacting with the world is the best way to beat the baby blues and start to feel good about yourself again.

I thought that the biggest learning curve would be with my first daughter and, for some things (diapers, breastfeeding, etc), it was. By the time she was one year old, things started falling into place. The routine got easier and Trinity was much more independent. As soon as that happened, I figured it must be time for another baby… and another. Now, with three beautiful girls, our family is complete.

My life as a Mom continues as a challenging, amazing journey.

Weekly trips to the zoo with my new mom friends were a great joy when I had Trinity. I needed that excuse to get up and get out of the house. The fresh air, exercise and company made a huge impact on my state of mind.

When my second daughter, Kayley, was five-months old, my husband and I achieved one of our goals of owning a business and purchased a retail wine and spirits store. I took on the full-time job of running the business while my husband kept his full-time job in the technology industry. With two babies and a business to run, things really started getting interesting! Why not add a second business and a third child? You know, I sure wouldn't want things to get boring, right?

There I was, overseeing a fledgling retail empire, just like I had always wanted. My husband and I had taken the step of getting a live-in nanny to help out, but even so, it was a challenge to keep my head above water. When I stepped back and took a look at my life, I realized that my dreams were different now. Owning a retail empire wasn't necessarily what I wanted anymore. So, I changed my life for the better and focused on what was truly important:

myself, my husband and my children. I am now proud to say that I am a stay-at-home mom (who happens to write the odd book on the side).

I have made choices, embraced changes and adapted my life to align with my current priorities. I have learned many things, and I have manifested incredible results and happiness in my life. I want to pass all of the goodies that I have learned on to you in this incredible package called "Be That Mom." Simple and instructional, Be That Mom will guide you in your journey to becoming the Mom that you want to be.

You don't have to be perfect. That is not what this is about. I simply want to encourage you to be happy with everything in your life, and I believe the strategies that I am going to share with you will help you achieve that. I want you to find calm, peacefulness and joy in being a Mom.

Remember, we are only given what we can handle, so rest assured that no matter what happens, you can handle it! Now, let's get started.

CHAPTER 1

Baby Mine

. . . .

Advice for the new mom/first-time mom

*"Being a Mother is not about what you gave up to have a child,
but what you've gained from having one."*
– Sunny Gupta

When Ryan and I first started dating, I was only 15 years old and he was 17. I always knew that I wanted to have children, and even at 15 I knew that Ryan would make a great dad. Being high school sweethearts, Ryan and I had a lot of time together to talk about our plans for having children. When was the right time to start having kids, how many will we have and what sex will they be (yes, for some reason we did think we could plan that!)? And, the grand old question... by what age should we be done having them? When it comes to having kids, even the best laid plans can get thrown out the window. Surprises and spontaneity are just a few of the amazing things that start happening more when you have children.

Ryan and I started trying for a baby about five years into our marriage. While it never seemed like a good time to start, after discussing it together, we thought it was as good a time as any. We were lucky that we got to make the choice at a time in our lives when we were ready (although after being together for so long, we had certainly been through our share of pregnancy scares!)

Both Ryan and I were working full time and we had become quite accustomed to our carefree lifestyle. We had disposable income from working, we had freedom to do what we wanted in the evenings and on weekends, and we had almost finished the renovations on our first condo, which was an ideal living space for the two of us. I could see why some people wait so long to start having children, but I could also see that the longer we decided to wait to have children, the harder that transition would be. The DINK lifestyle (double income, no kids) was easy to get used to!

But, all of a sudden, my internal clock started ticking. My plan was to be done having children by the time I was 30 years old. If that was going to happen, we needed to get busy! Ryan was a little nervous that we were "trying" to have a baby, however, being required to fulfill his "husbandly duties" on a regular basis was certainly appealing and exciting for him. To Ryan's dismay, it took only one month before I missed my monthly visitor.

Appropriately, it was the morning of Father's Day in June, 2005 when I first found out that I was pregnant. I got up before Ryan and made a quick trip to the drugstore for a pregnancy test and was anxiously peeing on that stick as soon as my bladder would let me. I remember watching expectantly, waiting for the appearance of those two telltale lines. It didn't take long before... a-ha! I was pregnant! I had butterflies in my tummy and a grin on my lips as I made my way up to our room, where Ryan was still asleep in our bed. I gently woke him up and announced that this was his first official "Father's Day."

The rest, as they say, is history. My belly grew, I ate lots of ice cream and I slept like I had been missing out on it for years. I worried, I stressed and I whined. Most of all, I could not wait for our sweet baby to arrive. Ryan supported me in every way. He picked up theatre popcorn and DQ blizzards, and anything else I was craving. He dried my tears when I cried at commercials and he helped me find the nearest washroom every time I needed it. He rubbed my back, my feet and anything else that needed rub-

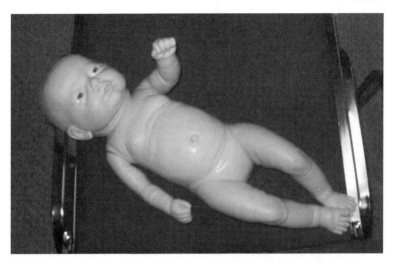

When we took our prenatal classes, this was one of the babies we got to practice on! Scary Baby! We had no idea what we were in for then... plastic baby training or not!

bing, and he made sure the nursery was ready months before we actually needed it. Pregnancy was an intense experience and at the time, I could not wait for it to be over. Little did I know that once my baby arrived, the real work would begin.

Exactly nine months later, Trinity blessed us with her presence.

Being the type of person I am, I set my expectations of motherhood high. I expected that becoming a mom would be easy and that it would come naturally for me. I had seen others do it (and I definitely passed judgment on them too harshly before I had walked a mile in their shoes). If all these other moms could do it, so could I. Of course, I would even do things better. Really, how hard could it be?

In my head, my house was always spotless and the laundry basket was never overflowing. My husband and I would eat delicious home-cooked meals together every evening while our baby cooed and giggled at us. I would work part-time, three-to-four hours per day, from home. I was going to have *soooo* much time on my hands.

Looking back now, I am not sure how I could have been so naïve and set myself up to fail so badly. I was in for a real shock! Nothing could have prepared me for the lack of sleep, the feedings every 20 minutes, or the intense amount of care that a baby required…from me! Trying to keep my house spotless and working part time in those early months drove me to exhaustion and made me extremely frustrated all the time. It took getting sick for me finally to call it quits on working. My baby needed me and I realized that I needed to start thriving instead of barely surviving.

I guess I believed that becoming a Mom would be a lot more ingrained, that biology would provide me with all of the skills I needed to care for another little person. But that's just not the case. There are a lot of things that biology just can't prepare you for. To illustrate to you how deep in the weeds I was my first time around, I'd like to share a hilarious little story:

I was having a hard time fitting in showering during the day and I expressed this to a group of new-mom friends. My friend Chrissy offered up the following advice: "Put your baby in the bouncy seat and bring her in the shower with you." It sounded like such an easy thing to do, and it was something I'd never considered trying. The following week, when we met again, I told Chrissy that I tried the shower thing, but I was frustrated because Trinity ended up getting soaking wet. "How do I keep my baby from getting wet?" I asked. Chrissy started howling with laughter. "Did you actually bring her right into the shower with you? I just meant for you to bring her into the bathroom with you, not right into the shower!" she said. I was so disoriented I hadn't even stopped to consider what she meant.

Realizing that I was far from perfect, and that I was fortunate to have choices in how I spent my time, I really started prioritizing my life to suit my own needs and I let everything else get taken care of in other ways. Creating my own dream "Mom" job was easy enough to do when I used the right tools and when I allowed myself to enjoy my new role. The tools were not easy to find, and they were not nicely displayed all in one place. I feel compelled to share here with you some of the tools that have worked for me. I trust these amazing tools will work for you also, and I hope you will be able to put them into practice immediately in your own life. Just remember, don't take your baby right into the shower with you unless you take them out of their sleepers first!

Baby mine... and yours — Though it will feel like you're fighting against your biological inclinations to never let your baby go or leave your sight, one of the healthiest things a new mom can do is learn to feel comfortable handing the baby over to a loved one. Giving yourself time away from your child, starting right from the time they are born, helps your child develop confidence that they will be okay without you. It also gives you some time to focus on you.

I recently attended a field trip with one of my daughters to a wildlife conservation area and I found it especially interesting to learn about the mother-and-offspring relationships among various animal species. The mother deer, for example, leaves her baby hidden alone in the grass while she takes the time to feed herself. This is also the case with the mother hare. These mothers always come back for their babies and, by taking care of themselves, making sure they are strong and well fed, they are then able to take better care of their babies.

This made me think about the days before people became accustomed to the cushy grocery store lifestyle. The days when we were required to fish, hunt and forage in order to survive. In these days, babies were in constant care, but not necessarily by the mother. The baby would often be strapped onto the back of a sister, auntie, or grandma, while the mother was engaged in food-gathering and other activities necessary for everyone's survival. There was a lot more support from extended families and fellow villagers or tribe members as far as childcare was concerned.

Even today, thriving as a mother requires support from others, either those within your own family, or other members of the community. I am fond of encouraging a little bit of separation between the mother and the child. When you continue to come back after short intervals of being away from your child, a trust relationship is formed. Your child knows that you are not abandoning them and they understand that you will always come back. In this way, your child will adapt to being held in the loving arms of other caring individuals.

If you are raising a child with a partner, it is important to give them time with the child when you are not around. First-time moms can often feel like they are the only ones who can properly take care of their own child, especially if the mother is nursing. But, if you are too clingy with your baby and you do not allow others to care for the baby, the baby will become dependent on you, exclusively, and will begin to refuse being cared for by others, or be less able to deal with having others care for them. This may seem like a good idea to any mom for the first three months, but eventually, Mama, trust me: you are going to need, and want, a break! It will get harder and harder the longer you prolong it... for you and for your baby.

"Baby-hogging" also leads to your partner being less confident in caring for the baby. If you do not allow your partner or spouse to assist, they will not learn how to do even the most basic of things. Bottle feedings, diaper changes — everything gets easier with practice. These days, dads and moms are sharing childcare duties more than ever. Some things are less innate for men, but that doesn't mean they shouldn't do those things, just that they need a bit more training and time. If you want help caring for your child, and you are lucky enough to have someone in your life that is willing to help, you have got to give them the opportunity to learn by just letting them go for it!

Your partner or spouse may be feeling extremely nervous about helping out because they, like you, are new at this and do not know what to do. No one likes the feeling of not knowing what to do. Insecurity can lead to feelings of fear, avoidance, anger and sadness. Perhaps that weird behavior your partner is exhibiting is just a result of "not-knowing syndrome." The only way this will change is if you give them an opportunity to learn.

Start with "baby steps," (sorry, I couldn't resist). Take a nice long shower or draw yourself a hot bath. Tune out for an hour and leave your partner in charge of the baby. Give them a few pointers without being condescending: "The baby just ate, so if she cries, she may need a diaper change, a nap or just a cuddle." Provide some encouragement before you go: "Thanks so much sweetie. I have been dying for a long bath. Enjoy your time with baby!" All too often, we want the help but we want to tell someone exactly how to do it, and we feel like it must be done our way. Do not make them feel afraid or nervous by saying things like: "Are you sure you'll be okay? I'll be really quick, so don't worry." This will make them feel like something terrible might happen. Instead, build their confidence by thanking them and then leaving things in their highly capable hands. Do this even if you're not totally feeling it. Fake it 'til you make it, I always say!

When you are done taking your little break, ask them, very calmly, how it went. If the baby has been screaming the whole time, try not to just rush over and take the baby like you are the only one with the tools to fix things (although, it's true that having lactating breasts does give you an unfair advantage). Ask them what they tried and perhaps give them a few pointers. Thank them again for the break and then ask them if they would like you to take the baby now.

The whole point is to build up their confidence as a caregiver to the child. Do not scold them or get upset if they don't know what they are doing, just provide guidance in a calm manner with some suggestions on how they can handle it next time. Sometimes your baby will just cry for no reason. That's just the way babies are. Sometimes the only thing you can do to avoid an emotional meltdown is to invest in a pair of earplugs.

Allowing your partner time with your child without you is also important so that they can learn how to do things their way.

This is an important point. Just because someone does something differently than you does not mean that way is wrong and your way is right. It just means that it is different. Different is good (within reasonable boundaries, of course). Instead of freaking out, pay attention — you just might learn something from watching how someone else handles your children.

It is also good for your child to learn different parenting and childcare styles. It will help your child be more understanding of the way things are in the real world. We all need to learn how to deal with change and with different ways of thinking. Change is the only constant in this life. You cannot raise your child in a bubble and then expect them to thrive in the outside world, which is where they will all, eventually, end up — whether you like it or not! The sooner you help them learn about change, the easier it will be for them. Let them learn within safe boundaries and they will grow into well-adjusted adults.

Another thing that can happen when you feel that you should be the only one to care for the children is that your partner or spouse can begin to feel left out. If you give all of your energy to your child, once the child is asleep, you will have no energy left for you or anyone else. Your partner needs some attention too. I always consider the mother-father relationship in this way: The two of you were here before the baby was born and you will still be there once your children fly the roost. If you do not nurture that relationship throughout your children's life, you run the risk of losing it.

Over the years, I have witnessed many couples do destructive things to their love relationships. Kicking your partner out of your marital bed so that you can sleep with your child should only be acceptable for the first few weeks after the birth, so that you can all survive the inevitably sleepless nights. But after that, you need to put a stop to it. How can you get the attention and affection you both need and deserve when there is a child in your bed every night? If you are no longer interested in sharing a bed with your spouse or partner, you need to start asking yourself why? Do not use your children as an excuse to avoid talking about or taking care of your relationship.

I have also seen parents who put absolutely all of their energy into their children as they grow, driving them everywhere and giving them every second of their spare time. Again, this can be a destructive situation for both the parent and the child. The child will come to expect that kind of attention from other people in their lives, which is completely unrealistic. Your child will be led to believe he or she is the only thing of any importance in their parents' lives. Though you may think that this is exactly what you want them to think, it is actually counterproductive.

Of course, you will dedicate a large portion of your time towards raising your children. I'm not suggesting in any way that you neglect them. That is not what this is about at all. It is about finding balance. If you give all of your attention to your children, what is left for you? Are you not the most important person in your own life? (The correct answer to this question is "yes"... YOU are the most important person in your life). If you are giving all of your time to your children, your own dreams, passions and pursuits are being put on the back burner. You might justify this by telling yourself that it is OK to put your life on hold until your children have moved out of the house... you'll get to it then...

In the meantime, opportunities are passing you by. Taking time for yourself all along your journey as a mom, to do things that you love or to learn new things, tells you that you care about yourself and that you are important enough to have time given to you. This, rather than self-sacrifice or constant doting, will bring you happiness and contentment. Your children will see the difference in how you feel about yourself!

So this is why it is so important to have others look after your baby for you — starting from a young age. Remember that they need to eventually live without you (as hard as that may be to think about at any age). You deserve to have time to nurture yourself, reconnect with the Universe and tell yourself you are worth it! You deserve to be fulfilled and happy every day. Don't look back with regret on your life by giving away precious time that you can never get back.

New Mom Survival Tips

Here are my top tips for new Moms to thrive during those tough first weeks:

1. Go with the flow. Allow your baby to set the schedule for those first 6 weeks, and allow yourself to work around your baby's schedule. Resist the urge to clean when your baby is sleeping. When they sleep, you should sleep too! Or at least do something healing and therapeutic, like taking a nice long shower.

2. Before you have your baby, stockpile some homemade cooling packs to deal with the after effects of the birth process. Buy thick maxi pads (regular old-school style, not those newfangled super-thin ones), a peri-care bottle and some calendula tincture (liquid calendula). Calendula can be found at your local health food store. Mix three drops of calendula tincture with water in your peri-care bottle. Line a cookie sheet with wax paper, or parchment paper and lay out as many maxi pads as will fit. Soak each pad with your calendula tincture, then place the tray of pads in the freezer. Once they are frozen (the next day), remove them from the cookie sheet and place them in Zip-loc bags. After you deliver your baby, use these as ice packs to help heal your bottom. They feel amazing after you have delivered your baby vaginally. They also really help with hemorrhoids. Keep your peri-bottle on hand in the bathroom and use warm water mixed with calendula to rinse yourself after using the toilet. The calendula is amazing for healing.

3. Feed yourself! Just like the mother deer, you need to take care of yourself first in order to provide proper care to your baby. Before you have your baby, stock the freezer with meals that are easy to just pull out and heat up. You can even ask people to

make food for you in lieu of a baby gift. In those first weeks, if people want to come and visit you (let's face it, they're coming to see the baby, not you), make it a requirement that they bring some kind of food. Even basic cooking can seem like an incredibly huge task in those first weeks, but the fact is that you will need to eat! Keep lots of fresh fruits, vegetables and healthy baking on hand so that you can easily feed yourself with one hand while you are feeding your baby.

4. When people come to visit, they will always ask if they can do anything for you. Instead of saying no, say: "Oh Yes! Please!" Getting someone to put in a load of laundry, or fold a bin of clean laundry and put it away can really take a load off your mind, and it will make your guest feel like they have done something special for you. Most people love to help, so accept help and actively ask for it, whenever you can.

5. Do not feel bad about restricting visitors in those first few weeks. If you are too tired, or overwhelmed, just say "no." If you can't say no yourself, designate a "gatekeeper," who will be able to politely decline on your behalf. Or simply do not answer the phone or door. Everyone will want to come over, but you need to be firm about what you want. When you have guests, you will feel compelled to tidy your house and be a good hostess, which may, or may not, be good for you and your baby. Use your own feelings as your guide and do only what feels right for you.

6. Free advice is worth only what you pay for it (as my Dad is known to say). As a first-time mom, everyone will be offering up advice and suggestions. Take their advice with a grain of salt, understand where it is coming from, say "thanks," and then take what you want from it. If it seems like it is going to work, do it! Try not to become annoyed when people start telling you what to do. They are only sharing advice because they think it will help. Remind yourself that their intentions are good, even if their advice is not.

7. What you say goes when it comes to your baby. No matter who is watching your baby, be sure they understand your rules

regarding your baby. Your own mother and mother-in-law will both have their own ideas about parenting – they raised you and your husband just fine, didn't they? But lots of things have changed over the course of the previous generation: babies don't sleep on their tummies, we use car seats, and baby walkers are no longer considered safe, for starters. You must stand your ground and be up front with anyone who watches your baby. If you don't allow soothers or bottles, make sure people know that. If you want people to wash their hands before they hold your baby, make that your rule and stick to your guns! While people may whisper under their breath about what an overprotective mom you are, remember that what other people think about you is none of your business! Do what you feel is best for you, your baby and your family, regardless of what others think.

8. Find a couple of friends with babies who are the same age. Public healthcare offices often host "new mom" groups on a weekly basis, which is a good place to start. This is a great way to meet other moms, who most likely live close by. The Moms101 class that I attended was my lifesaver! You'll realize that other moms are going through the same kind of things that you are going through. It's helpful to hear about other people's experiences. You are not alone!

9. Read! When your baby is breastfeeding, have a good book on hand. Read parenting books, or just some good smutty chick lit or a trashy gossip magazine. It's a way to stimulate your mind and also relax while you are feeding your baby.

10. Get out of the house once a day. Make this a rule. This will force you to at least get dressed and do your hair, even if you don't have time for a shower. If you just take a walk around the block, the fresh air and change of scenery will do wonders for your mood. At first, it can be overwhelming to get yourself and your baby ready to get out of the house. Keep your diaper bag packed and ready to go at all times with extra diapers, a change of clothes, wipes, and water and snacks for you. Replenish it at

the end of every day so that you will have less to do when you're getting ready to go out the next day.

Did you know you can make your own baby wipes? Be That Green Mom! Chemical free, easy to make, reusable and cost effective, making your own bum wipes can be awfully rewarding. All you need is a stack of face cloths (can be older, as long as there is still some wiping surface left), and an airtight container to fit them in. Thanks to Diva Diapers (www.divadiapers.com) I am able to provide you with details on making homemade wipes.

Here are their recommendations (reprinted with permission):
Whenever possible, use all-natural ingredients. Most ingredients are available at health food stores. It's fun to experiment and come up with your own recipe too, by mixing & matching ingredients from the different wipe solution recipes, or adding your own special touch.

Please keep in mind that if you're treating diaper rash, it's best to use plain water.

Main Ingredients

Water: Best to use distilled. Tap water goes moldy quickly.

Soap: Baby shampoo is a favorite, but baby wash, or liquid soap (like Castile) are also recommended.

Oil: Usually baby oil. You can also use Olive Oil.

Fragrance & Other: Essential oils are used both for their fragrance and other intrinsic properties specific to each oil (i.e. tea tree oil-antibacterial). Vinegar is said to help slow down mold growth.

General Methods

For dry wipes: Simply mix the ingredients into a spray bottle. You can either spray the wipe and use it wet or spray the baby's bottom for a mini bidet treatment. The solution may also be kept in a jar and cloth wipes dipped in it.

For wet wipes: You can use an empty commercial wipes container or any plastic container with a lid. Mix the ingredients in a separate container. Place the wipes in the container, then add the solution, and invert a few times to make sure the wipes all get sufficiently moistened. Use just enough solution to moisten. Extra solution can generally be kept refrigerated.

For dry wipes with water only: Keep dry wipes in diaper change area and wet under tap water when ready to use. This method works particularly well for baby's with extra sensitive skin.

Original Recipe for Wipes

1/8-1/4 c. baby shampoo

1/8-1/4 c. baby oil/olive oil

2 cups lukewarm water

Mix liquid ingredients gently and use with your preferred method.

Basic Wipes #1

1 -3 cups water

1/8 cup baby oil or olive oil

3-5 drops tea tree oil

8 drops lavender oil

Shake gently with 1/8 cup baby shampoo.

Basic Wipes #2

2 cups water

2 T. baby oil or olive oil

1 T. baby bath

1-2 drops Tea Tree oil

1-2 drops Lavender oil

Anti-Fungal Baby Wipes

1/2 c. distilled water

1 tsp. vinegar

1/4 c. aloe vera gel

1 TBS. calendula oil

1 drop lavender essential oil

1 drop tea tree essential oil

Simple Anti-Fungal Wipes

2 cups (16 oz) water

2-5 drops Tea Tree oil

2-5 drops Lavender oil

1 tsp. of your favorite baby wash (optional)

*see notes below

Herbal Wipes

2 cups water

2 tsp. baby shampoo

1/4 cup aloe vera gel

1 tbsp. calendula oil

3 drops tea tree essential oil

3 drops lavender essential oil

Calendula Wipes

2 cups water

2 tsp. baby shampoo

1/4 cup aloe vera gel

1 tbsp. calendula oil

5 drops lavender essential oil

5 drops tea tree essential oil

Lanolin Wipes

4 cups water

1 tbsp baby shampoo, baby wash, or liquid soap

1-3 drops essential oil

1/4 tsp pure liquid lanolin

1 tbsp. liquid glycerin

Castile Wipes

1 cup water

1 tbsp. Baby Dr. Bronner's liquid castile

1 tbsp. baby oil or olive oil

2 drops tea tree essential oil

5 drops lavender essential oil

Aloe Vera Wipes

1 cup distilled water

1/2 cup aloe vera gel

2 tbsp. calendula oil

2 drops tea tree essential oil

2 drops lavender essential oil

2 tbsp. Witch Hazel

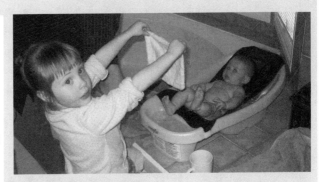

Clean your baby naturally!

Fun with Baby

My sister-in-law, Debra, is one of the most amazing Moms out there! With four wonderful children (all in their teens) and a background assisting and educating parents in the early stages of parenthood, Debra is a great resource for ideas about fun stuff to do with kids.

What I've noticed most about Debra as I watched her raising her own children over the years was that she had a consistent focus on having fun. Parenting is a lot more rewarding when you and your children are happy! Babies don't just need to eat, poop and sleep, they also like to be stimulated with fun things — even if they only have a five-minute attention span! That said, "fun" with a baby is a little different than having fun with an older child.

Here are a few easy things that I've learned from Debra, and others, that will help you have fun with your baby and also help stimulate brain development (moms love multi-tasking!):

- Make your own baby toys (or at least play with the ones you have on hand). Spend a few minutes every day, when your baby is fed, alert and not yet tired and show your child the toys and talk to them about the toy, or the pictures on it, or just about your day! As soon as your baby no longer takes interest (looks away or cries) then playtime is over. Your baby's attention span will increase over time, but in the beginning, you may only "play" for a few minutes at a time. Soon enough, your baby will be asking you for play time and will cry when you stop playing peek-a-boo! Check out **www.bethatmomnow.com** for some cool instructions on making your own stimulating baby toys with some simple household materials.

*Stimulating toys do not have to be expensive or complicated. Black and white patterns are best for young babies, so keep it simple when it comes to toy making. Debra helped make toy boxes like these during her career with the Family First program in Manitoba. See the website (**www.bethatmomnow.com**) for details on creating these for your baby!*

- Singing and talking to your baby, as well as repeating rhymes with actions, is very stimulating for them. You can dig up some of the songs or rhymes from your own childhood, but chances are, as a first time mom, it's been a while since you sang *"Momma's going to buy you a mockingbird..."* Don't be discouraged if you can only remember one verse, or if you think you have a terrible voice. Remember that you are someone's mommy, and your voice will always be their favorite one to hear, no matter what it sounds like. I encourage you to sing a song or recite a rhyme to your baby every day. Debra has been kind enough to pass on a booklet that included a compilation of some classic favorites, as well as some rhymes and songs you may never have heard of, but that will be new classics for you and your kids. Check out **www.bethatmomnow.com** to download a free copy of this compilation booklet for yourself!
- Read books to your baby. Reading is important bonding time for parents and children, and an essential way to inspire a love of reading at a young age. You can read any kind of books to your baby, and you can start while they are still in your tummy! You are never too young or too old to enjoy a good book! Again, realize that your voice is incredibly soothing to your child so they will find this to be a pleasant experience (and reading together usually involves some bonus lap-cuddle time). You will bond with your kids and learn things together through reading. Make frequent trips to the library if you get bored of reading the same books over and over again (but rest assured, there will come a day when having memorized Margaret Wise Brown's *Goodnight Moon*, or *One Fish Two Fish Red Fish Blue Fish* by Dr. Seuss, will come in handy).
- Get down on the floor. Babies spend a lot of time on the floor during their first year. Get down there with them, crawl around at their level, play with blocks, and lay with them when they are having tummy time. As adults, we tend not to spend much time on the floor, but it is important to sometimes be at the same

level as your child. Perhaps you will be inspired practice a few yoga poses or do a little meditation while you're down there? It certainly couldn't hurt.

While the first year of your baby's life will inevitably be very challenging, try your best to enjoy every moment — even the sleepless, crying ones! Your baby will not stay a baby for long. The sweet, fat, baby rolls and sleepless nights will make way for toddler antics and other adventures. While it may be hard to believe right now, one day you will miss having a crying, cooing little angel in your arms.

As moms, sometimes we want to rush our children on to the next stage, phase or age. How many times have you heard a fellow mom say something like: "I can't wait until he is sleeping through the night!" or, "I can't wait until she is crawling!" or, "It will be so nice to be done with diapers!" I encourage you to live vibrantly in every moment, even the tough, tired, frustrated moments, and force yourself to smile often. Your baby will grow up faster than you can imagine, so don't take this precious time for granted. When you find yourself missing the baby phase, it is probably a sign that you're ready to have another one — if that is in the cards for you!

God sure knew what he was doing when he made babies so absolutely adorable. Those sweet little faces make it all worthwhile.

CHAPTER 2

Planet Do It!

· · · · · · · · · · · · · · ·

"Do what feels right. Live your life for you and no one else. Make changes when it doesn't feel right. The goal is not to be perfect, the goal is to be happy."
–Tina O'Connor

So... you're a mom! Now what??!!

I have always told myself that I could never be a stay-at-home mom. That simply was not the kind of person I believed I was. But life can be unpredictable and now I am just that — completely by choice, I might add. Be careful how you talk to yourself, or you will start believing it! At the very least, you will limit yourself and your thinking…or you may expand yourself and find that the world can really be your oyster!

How you define success for yourself is all that matters. My idea of success used to be me out working hard, pursuing my own career as a business owner, with a nanny helping out at home and I achieved that. I had everything I always wanted. But then I stood back and watched my children growing up from afar and I realized that I had to make a change. After eight years of having someone help me raise my children while I ran my own businesses, I immersed myself back into my family.

Realize that as you grow and time passes, the things that are important to you change as well. Constantly analyze your priorities and make sure you are doing things that feel good to you. Don't just keep doing the same thing because it used to be okay, or it's always been that way. Follow your passions... not your pensions, and you too will be amazed at what happens in your life.

The goal is not to be PERFECT as a mom. The goal is to be happy and enjoy what you have and what you do. Happiness is a choice. If you are not feeling happy, you have only 2 choices...

    1. Choose to feel differently about your current situation.

    2. Change your current situation.

Remember, you have ultimate control over your life. Are you ready to start planning your life instead of letting nature take its course?

Planet Do It!

My husband Ryan and I have a long running joke that we are from "Planet Do It." We have always been able to "plan", and then just "do" things...and we would like to invite you to be from Planet Do It too!

I once received a fortune in a cookie at my favorite Chinese restaurant that rang true. It clearly stated the way I feel about getting what you want out of life:

"Good luck is the result of great planning"

When you take 'luck' out of the equation you become responsible for your life. It is very easy to blame the results you are getting in your life on external forces — good luck, bad luck, the phase of the moon, hormones, karma... but in the end, if you realize that you are the master of your domain, and your life, you will unleash a power within yourself that you may not have known existed. You ARE in control of your life, your destiny, and your luck.

Empower yourself with the truth about your life and you'll realize that you may be where you are in spite of yourself. This realization can easily change your life by creating a "plan" to get where you really want to be.

Sounds simple, right? Sure, but first you have to get over yourself and that can be the hardest part. If you already know where you want to be, what would you want to do? What would you like to have in life? If you are going to create a plan to get somewhere or to have/do something, you have got to know where you are going and what you intend to do when you get there. Knowing this is key.

I have created the Planet Do It exercise to help you dream and create the life that YOU want for yourself. This exercise will take approximately 15 minutes of your time. I encourage you to gift yourself 15 extra minutes today, to do something incredible for yourself. Please love yourself enough to not only read through this exercise, but actually DO this exercise. You are worth it. This could be a real life changer for you — *why wait to change your life?*

How you define yourself is who you are.

Think about this one for a minute:

"You may well know me by now. My name is Tina. I am a beautiful, confident, successful, sassy, powerful, and incredible woman who lives to inspire and organize!"

I *am* all of these things because I tell myself I am these things... not the other way around! Keep that in mind.

Now, it is time to be honest with yourself. Really, really honest. This is about what you want. Not what your parents want for you, or what your partner wants for you or what your boss wants for you. It's not about what's best for your kids. And it is definitely not about what you think would be sensible or the best way to pay the bills. This is all about your *dreams*. What is it that you long for? What are your aspirations? Your goals? What do you feel is missing in your life? What do you want to improve? What would you like to change? You need to be specific here and you need to be personal. It's time to RE-define YOU!

We'll begin by breaking things down. Grab some paper — any kind of paper will work for now. I want this to be easy for you and I want you to be able to do it right now. Two sheets of paper should do it. At the end of this book, you will find several blank pieces of paper that you can use for this exercise. No excuses! Do it NOW!

It is important that you do not feel too overwhelmed, so let's just focus on six areas in your life. Copy the following list down, leaving a good amount of space between each item to accommodate more writing.

1. **Relationships**
   a.
   b.
   c.
2. **Travel**
3. **Career**
4. **Money**
5. **Self**
6. **Things**

When you first start, your plan should look like this.

Don't start writing anything more just yet, simply sit and think for a moment about what you would like to improve/ change/have in those six areas of your life? Don't worry about the status quo, or whether you think you can or cannot actually have, or do, the things you want. This is a fantasy assignment. Be ridiculous with your thoughts about what you can or could have. Stretch the Universe and your own ability to create what you want.

Remember:
"Whatever the mind of man can conceive and believe, it can achieve." – W. Clement Stone

Allow yourself to believe in something a little out there…a little crazy, a little wild, and a lot of fun! ANYTHING goes at this point — Anything!

I have provided you with some ideas to inspire you. Feel free to use any of the ideas listed here. Change them to suit your needs or just copy them as is. But, be sure to connect to them in a personal way. If nothing resonates with you personally, do not write it down. The one thing I must make you aware of is to be as specific as you possibly can when you write these goals down . If you are looking to make more money, state the amount; if you want to travel, say where you want to go.

1. Relationships
- I want to find a partner who is my best friend and wants to do everything with me.
- I want to improve my relationship with my parents.
- I want to have a closer relationship with my children.
- I want to improve my relationship with my partner…more intimacy, better communication, more teamwork.
- I want to reconnect with my long-lost best friend, or find a new one.
- I want to improve my relationships with my co-workers, or boss(es).

2. Travel
- I want to travel to anywhere outside the town where I live.
- I want to travel anywhere outside of the country where I live.
- I want to travel around the world with my kids!

- I want to travel around the world without my kids too.
- I want to go to (insert place) for the weekend (or for a week, or a year...).
- I want to travel to Italy (and while I am there, I might just buy a vineyard for the summers).
- I want to walk into the airport in the middle of the day with no luggage and get on the next flight out to wherever I want, and then buy everything I need when I get there!
- I want to take my kids to Disneyland.
- I want to go on a cruise to Alaska and then Barbados.

3. Career/Education

- I want to quit my crummy job. I am unhappy.
- I want a promotion within my company.
- I want to find a job that pays me (insert amount) per year/hour/month.
- I want to work for a boss or an organization that appreciates and respects the job I do, but also has its fun moments.
- I want to start my own business. (If you know what type of business you want, such as a floral shop, write that down. Otherwise just leave it open).
- I don't want to work anymore. I want to stay home and raise my children.
- I want to upgrade and get my high-school diploma.
- I want to go back to school and become a (fill in the blank).
- I want to make (insert amount) per month working from home.
- I want to take a sabbatical and work in a beach cabana in Australia for a few months.
- I want to go to take Spanish lessons in Spain...Spanish in the morning, wine in the afternoon! (Create your own to suit you!)

4. Money

- I want to make (insert amount) per year in my job.
- I want to get a raise (any amount will do or specify an amount).
- I want $50,000 for a down payment to an Italy vineyard.

- I want $100,000 for a shopping spree on Rodeo Drive with my mom and my sister.
- I want $5,000 to take my kids to Disneyland.
- I want to help others by donating a portion of my income and time.
- I want to have a bank account that just keeps replenishing itself every time I take something out of it!

5. Self

- I want to be less stressed, have more fun and be more relaxed.
- I want to lose weight (or gain weight).
- I want to be healthier and have more energy.
- I want to do more yoga (or hiking, or join a softball team or tennis club, or horseback riding).
- I want to go for a pedicure every month and have cute-looking toes all the time.
- I want to play golf Wednesday and Friday mornings before work and Tuesday and Thursday evenings after work.
- I want to read my book for one hour every Sunday.
- I want to hire a housecleaner.
- I want to have gorgeous hair and skin.
- I want to wake up feeling rested and excited about my day every morning.

6. Things

- I want a downtown high-rise condo.
- I want a house on an acreage. (or close to downtown...)
- I want an expensive new sports car (or a vintage '68 Ford Mustang).
- I want a pair of Jimmy Choo's... and a pair of Manolo's,...wait make that a few pairs of each and a large, walk-in closet to store them in.
- I want a diamond ring, of the engagement variety, or for no reason at all.
- I want a new set of golf clubs and some cute golf outfits.
- I want a motorbike. Wait, make that a cool new stroller!

- I want a car that's reliable.
- I want a vineyard in Italy for the summer, a beach house in Barbados for the winter, and a Yacht to take me anywhere else I might want to go the rest of the year.
- I want a house/condo/apartment that is all MINE!
- I want a new computer.
- I want a dog, or a cat.
- I want a housekeeper who will prepare healthy meals for my family. I also want a gardener, a personal trainer, a masseuse, and a private tutor for my children.
- I want it all. I am a woman!

Okay, now it's your turn now. Take a moment to think about each of those areas in your life — *only a moment, though* — and then just let your ideas spill out. Feel free to "poach and merge" anything from my list, just make sure it is really something you want. Write as much as you can under each category without passing judgment about whether you can or cannot do these things, or what it would take to do these things. Break down all the walls that you have built up over time about who, or what you are, and allow yourself to be redefined in your own mind. Make sure you think of *at least one thing* for each category before you move on and don't worry about how many things you have. This is not a contest. The more specific and honest you are, the better off you will be.

Allow yourself to write things down even if you do not have the specifics mapped out in your head just yet. For example, say you want to start your own business, but you do not know what kind of business it would be? Write down your motivation to start one and we'll work on the rest later. Do not allow yourself to think of why you cannot do these things. For now let's pretend that there is nothing holding you back from what you want to do. Literally, for the time being, consider that you have hit the life jackpot and you can now do anything. Think as if there are no restrictions, no fear and no limitations. The more outrageous that you allow yourself to be with this exercise, the more you are opening yourself up to the infinite possibilities of you. Be ridiculous!

As Dr. Seuss once said:

"Fantasy is a necessary ingredient in living, it's a way of looking at life through the wrong end of a telescope, which is what I do, and that enables you to laugh at life's realities. I like nonsense, it wakes up the brain cells."

So, here we are. Did you really do this task? *Really?* Did you actually write stuff down? If so, I am proud of you! This is an important step toward making a change. If not, please consider doing it now. Writing down your hearts desires with your own hand helps to reinforce these desires and gets your subconscious working for you. It will make such a difference... I can wait — so go for it! I am so excited for you! Take your time, focus, and allow all your inner desires to surface before your eyes.

How do you feel after writing all those things down? I hope you feel exhilarated.

Now, for the real challenge. Read over your list and pick the one thing (only one for now) from each category that excites you the most and that you want the most. Again, be honest with yourself. This is about you and no one else. Do not limit yourself, or think about what it would take to possibly accomplish these things. Just choose the thing that feels good way down deep inside. Mark each of those items with a little star(*) or heart!

I would like you to start with a clean, fresh, new sheet of paper. Track down a favorite pen that writes nicely or is your favorite color. This will be your "good copy," so give it the attention it deserves. In the top right hand corner of your clean sheet of paper, write today's date in small letters. Then, as your title, I want you to write (insert your name)'s Five Year Plan. Below that, but still at the top of the page, write the following: "I am so happy and proud of myself that I have, or have accomplished, all of these things."

Next, I want you to transfer the six starred items from your initial worksheet onto the nice clean sheet with the date. You are going to rewrite each item on your list in the present tense, rather than the future tense. Instead of "I want" or "I wish," write "I have," or "I am doing..." pretend that you already have, or are doing these things right now. For example, "I want to travel to Italy" becomes "I am travelling to Italy this year" or "I want a raise of $10,000 per year" becomes "I got a raise of $10,000"! List your six items in whatever order you like.

Now, I want you to read over those six items, in your head, and then out loud. Wow! You just created a 5 year plan in 30 minutes or less! Look at all of your goals and dreams and aspirations — You really are the kind of person that knows what they want in life.

At this point, you may choose to be done with your plan. But, if you like you can embellish your page with stickers or pictures or drawings — anything that makes it feel special and personal to you. Flip through some magazines and cut out pictures of things that you desire (such as vineyards, shoes, diamonds, men, kids, boats, money, cars, beaches, clothes etc), and glue them onto your plan. You may simply choose to draw a happy face, or some hearts, or add some sparkly, pretty stickers that make you feel happy (seriously, it's fun and it makes you feel like a kid again). Go all out and add borders and frames or choose to keep it simple. This is about what you want, so don't worry about what others would

Make your plan personal to you, and then be accountable to it. This is your life, and you deserve to fulfill yourself in every way!

do. Your plan should reflect your own personal style and it should feel good to you at this point in your life.

Keep the original worksheet of your plan as well. I feel that it is important to focus you by charting a course for just those things that really resonate with you…those things that give you butterflies in your tummy when you think about them. The more you focus your attention on a smaller number of things that you feel emotionally attached to, the more easily you will manifest those things. If you feel broken hearted about leaving something behind that you originally wrote down on the rough draft, then by all means, please add it to your good copy. As long as you have at least one thing from each of the 6 categories, just do whatever feels right after that. Only you know what you want and how quickly you want it. This plan is not fixed. The only sure thing in this life is change, so expect to make revisions to your plan over time as new things happen.

Don't worry... Change is good!

For this next step, I would like you to decide where you will keep your plan in your home. This is a personal choice. If you are a private person, you may choose to fold up your plan and tuck it in your underwear drawer. If you are someone who wants to share her dreams, you might want to pin it up on the wall of your office or beside the calendar in the kitchen, or to post it on Facebook for the world to see. Be accountable - put it somewhere you won't forget about it. Do what feels right to you. Just seeing your plan often, even if it is folded, will remind your subconscious about your dreams and keep you moving forward. That is why I suggest your underwear drawer…I do hope you go in there once a day!

This is not to say you have to read it over every day — reading it every few months will keep you accountable. When you review your plan, take a good look at the date. Assess where you are in relation to your goals. Make sure you are taking action. You know what you want. Are you on track to get it? Only you will know that for sure.

I know, I know. You have questions. "How will I achieve these goals? I was just writing down a bunch of stuff... I didn't actually think about realizing those goals. It all seems so unrealistic."

Stop that silly self-defeating talk for now and for good. Remember how empowering it felt to write those things down? Let's hang on to that feeling and just imagine yourself doing, having and improving on all those things from that list. How does that feel? Pretty good, right? Of course it does! If you stay focused on what you want, and enjoy every moment of the journey, you are going to get to where you're going. The Universe will make sure you get there. The surprising thing is usually in the "how am I going to get there?", and believe me it doesn't always happen the way you think it will. This is where, as George Michael sings "You just gotta have faith!" When you know where you're going, you believe in your-self, and you have faith, suddenly opportunities seem to just land on your plate. You will have to make choices about what to do with the opportunities that come your way...will you eat them or toss them? My advice...if it feels good, do it (*even if you shouldn't*, Sloan's advice, not mine, but it still may be applicable!)

Now that you know what you want, you are ready to start making some other exciting changes. Let's keep going with the next phase of your "Mom" Makeover!

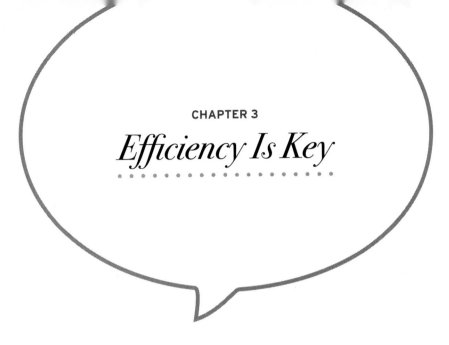

CHAPTER 3

Efficiency Is Key

. . . .

"We may be very busy, we may be very efficient, but we will only be truly effective when we begin with the end in mind."
–Stephen R. Covey

Efficiency is the ability to get the maximum done in the least amount of time. One of the key elements to being efficient, is learning how to schedule your time so that your life can run smoothly, successfully, and in accordance with your priorities.

To be efficient, relaxed and happy, you must maximize the time you have while reducing the worrying you do. To get yourself on the efficiency train, you will need two things:

1. An agenda or calendar (hard copy or digital).
2. A notebook or journal . (In this case, I prefer hard copy. There is something magical that happens when you write with your own hand.)

This all starts with you taking the time to schedule yourself, then taking time to review that schedule, and adjust as needed. When you know what is coming next, it is easy to feel relaxed about the days and weeks ahead, and to enjoy today more because you are not worrying about the unknown future. Doing a simple thing like scheduling and reviewing your schedule will make you feel prepared and relaxed.

You will also need a place to keep track of your thoughts, ideas and inspirations as they come. Your brain may be running with your next big idea just as you are in the middle of something else. You will need to maintain your focus on the task at hand, while also not losing sight of that big idea! Writing things down as they come to mind relieves the anxiety you may have about forgetting those important thoughts. All of us are guilty of having our attention on one task pulled away by some new and exciting thought. I would encourage you to write the new idea in your notebook or journal, and then get back to the task at hand. As more time becomes available, you can go back and review your notebook and decide what your next priority should be.

Here are some **tried-and-true** time management tips that I use every day:

- Create a daily schedule for yourself that is broken down into half-hour increments. You can buy an agenda that is laid out this way, or if you are impatient like me and want to "do it now," you can simply print out a daily, or weekly calendar from Outlook or another computer program and keep your sheets in a three-ring binder. This system will allow you to keep track of pretty much everything you do over the course of the day.
- Keep your schedule binder with you at all times. You can make "to-do" lists and notes right there on each day's page. This allows you to see exactly what kind of time you have in a day to schedule the appointments, events and activities that need to get done.
- In order to feel prepared and on-track, schedule simple household chores and other every day activities. Things like doing the laundry, meal preparations and buying groceries should all be in

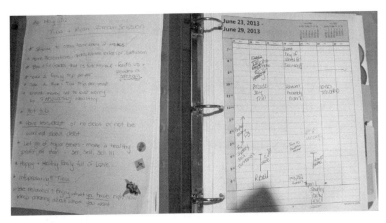

Here is a sample of my agenda. As you can see, I also keep my "Planet Do-it" right where I can see it every day. Ryan and I created this "plan" in May of 2012, and we've already checked off quite a few!

the schedule. Include driving time and try to be realistic about what you can actually get done in a day. Hair appointments, work hours, workouts, play dates, lunches, vacations, volunteer days and deadlines should all be in there. *Everything* you do in a day should be on your list. This includes work, family and personal time.

- Schedule in your personal time and do your best to not allow anything to interfere with your time. YOU are important - while it is imperative that you care for your family, you must also take care of you to be able to do that efficiently. It's easy to schedule in a yoga class that you attend outside of the house every week, as there is a set time, and you are paying for it (amazing how when you've paid for something it suddenly increases the priority). But what about the yoga that you 'd like to do at home, or the reading you'd like to do, or the online class you've been wanting to take? How about coffee with friends, or painting your nails or going for a leisurely walk? What about that gym membership you bought last year? Golf, soccer, gardening... what have you been missing out on because you haven't allowed yourself the time for? If you are constantly saying "I have no time for myself...my family is too busy", it's time to TAKE some time back. Reward yourself for all your hard work daily by prioritizing YOU!

- Try to avoid using different calendars for your family. It is way too hard to keep track of both and it requires a lot of time! You can easily set up a Google calendar online that can be shared with your partner and your children. This is a great solution for busy families who are technologically skilled. You can add your own events in one color, your partner can add theirs in one color, and your kids can all have different colors. You can still print off hard copies of this calendar to keep with you, or access it through your Smartphone while you are out and about.

- Set your mind at ease by reviewing the next day before you go to bed at night. Perhaps at this point you'll notice an extra hour somewhere. What are you going to do with that hour? Is it enough time to squeeze in a trip to the grocery store? Would you rather get a quick pedicure, or just relax and read a book? Perhaps it would be a good time to take care of something with an upcoming deadline like renewing your Driver's license.

You will have the time to do everything you want if you learn to schedule your time and if you prioritize based on your needs. If you find that you are just simply not able to complete certain tasks, or it seems you never have enough time, then it's possible you do not want the result bad enough. Results come through actions and sometimes we have to do things that we do not like in order to get the desired results. Prioritize your tasks according to how quickly you want to see results. Also, you may need to "let go" of some things in order to "buy" yourself more time for other things. You need to do things that you enjoy and that add positivity to your life. Allow yourself to say NO to certain things that are not important to you and you will open up windows of time for things that you DO value! Remember that this is your life and what others think about what you do is none of your business.

So make choices that work for you, and don't be influenced by what others think. You are the one ultimately responsible for your life, so you GET to make the choices for YOU. Let go of any guilt you may be harboring about anything and embrace your own freedom of choice.

When you write down something you absolutely need to do, try to be diligent about doing it now, or at least very soon! Be accountable to yourself and do not let yourself down. Of course, this means you will have to be reasonable about how much you can get done in a day. There is only so much time. If you are being realistic, however, you should be able to fit in whatever you need to do as long as you do not waste your time.

Change is inevitable, and life is often unpredictable; however, on the whole humans do best when life has some structure to it. Humans enjoy having routine and knowing "What's up next?" on the schedule. As soon as you think: "Oh, I should really do that," (like "I should plan that birthday party," or "I should schedule my doctor's appointment," or "I should book summer camps for the kids") write this intention down in your agenda or notebook. But instead of using "I SHOULD", write " I WILL". This will take it out of your head and get you, and the Universe, working on it right away.

Set deadlines for yourself. Otherwise, you'll never have a reason to get things done because really, most of what we do can always be done later. If you set a date for when you want something completed, you will know how much time you have to complete it and you can start breaking that project down in terms of how much you have to get done to reach your goal. If you set a date, do everything in your power to stick to it. You need to be accountable to your goals.

Teamwork — Two heads are better than one…imagine what 4 or 6 could do? Form your team at home! 'That Mom' shouldn't have to do it all on her own! You have got to use teamwork in every area of your life. If you are consistently thinking about functioning as a team, whether it is at work or at home or at the gym, you will be more efficient and so will the people around you. It's win-win all around!

Teaching teamwork at home is an important part of being 'That Mom'. You can encourage your family to help out as a team, making it a positive, exciting event. You are part of something more...you belong to a group of people that works *together* to have fun and enjoy life to the fullest. There will always be maintenance in any home, it takes effort to feed yourself, and keep the space you live in neat and clean. Encourage your children, and anyone else that lives in the home, to put their teamwork hats on around the house at all times. Children are extremely good at helping out around the house, as long as you ask them to do it! If you make it a given, or a rule, that everyone helps out and does their part for the good of the team (Go Team O'Connor!), you children will respond accordingly.

Don't feel bad asking your kids, or your partner, to help out. There should be no guilt surrounding rounding your family up to help out the team. Helping is involvement. Everyone wants to be involved, especially in such an amazing family! Make it fun to help out.

So, what can your children be expected to do at home? Well, pretty much everything, at a certain age! If you start training them young, you'll have a hard working staff of children by the time they are about 9! In all seriousness, it will take longer for the bathroom to get cleaned when your kids are 4 and 6 years old, and you will have to supervise this event, which means you are still basically doing it! But, over time, you will be able to delegate tasks to your team, and you won't have to be there to help! Plus, if you have trained them well, they will be able to do the tasks up to your standards. Delegation and training take time initially, but you get it all back and more in the long run. Take time to help your children learn HOW to help you. They like to do things right, and they like to be good at things, and get your praise and respect. What better way to get that than through a few household chores!

As with any activity, try to keep their chores age appropriate. Using non-toxic, chemical free home cleaners makes it even more easy to allow your children some freedom with the cleaning products.

Here are a few ways you can get your team working in the home:

- Cleaning Bathrooms – You can get them to take everything off the counters and out of the shower or bath and put it outside the bathroom. You can give them their own spray bottles, and rags and let them go to town in your bathroom! Be sure to supervise, and teach them how to use the toilet brush properly so they can scrub away those stains the way you want 'em. Nice sparkly toilet bowls are awesome.
- Vacuuming and sweeping floors.
- Loading and Unloading the dishwasher.
- Doing the dishes, and putting them away.

It's not the most fun job there is, but your kids don't have to know that!
Teach them the value of a "fresh bowl" and help them learn how to get it!

Everyone can help to load and unload the dishwasher. It's much easier to do that then have to wash and dry and put away all of the dishes without a dishwasher. Keep it in perspective!

Weekly garbage maintenance can be a family affair if you are willing to ask for help. It's amazing what kids can do to help out!

Now that is some serious teamwork! Those Rice Krispie squares turned out so well and the girls had a blast. When you work together, you can create amazing things!

- Setting and clearing the table. Start them off small with just the plates and progress by adding items until they can do the whole thing themselves. With clearing, you may start by asking everyone to at least clear their own plate to the kitchen. Then progress to everyone has to take at least 1 extra thing from the table.
- Watering plants. Kids love this one! Young ones will need lots of supervision, but you'll get 'em trained.
- Cooking. Not only is cooking a fun event for kids, cooking is an essential life skill that your child will use every day to keep themselves healthy. You are never too young to start learning kitchen skills. Measuring, chopping, washing veggies, getting out tools and ingredients for you, even just watching what you do is a great way to get your kids involved.
- Baking. You and your children will enjoy the journey of baking almost as much as the sweet treats you end up with!

Baking is science! The right amounts of the right ingredients can earn you a delicious, hot out of the oven treat! Creating cookies that your kids can use cookie cutters with takes longer, due to refrigeration time, but they are totally worth it! Making shapes with cookie dough is one of the most fun parts about baking cookies.

Cookies Are Done – Amazingly, we ended up having enough candies to decorate our cookies with. Another great part about baking is eating that raw cookie dough and any sweet decorations... just to be sure that they pass the kid quality test.

- Preparing grocery lists and meal plans. Involve your family in deciding what they would like to eat, and have them help you create grocery lists. They can go searching in the pantry for you to see if you have cornflake crumbs for your recipe, or be writing things on the list once they are able. Teaching them how to plan for meals and run an organized home can start as early as you are ready.
- Laundry! Kids are totally able to do their own laundry if you are willing to teach them. I have a laundry bin in each of my kids rooms, and only their clothes go in their baskets (It is way too difficult to tell my 3 girls' clothes apart!). Everything can pretty much be washed together when they are younger, and as they get older you can teach them to sort by color. When they are young, get them putting their own clothes into the washer, and helping with soap and turning it on. When the clothes are washed, let them help you hang them to dry or have them move the clothes to the dryer and turn it on. Teach them to fold their own clothes. If folding is too much for them, you can do the folding, place the items (sorted) on their beds, and have them put the clothes away in the right places. They can do it, if you let them!

Be That Mom Laundry Tip: The Missing Sock Bag Game! Finding socks used to be such an annoyance in our house. Everyone would have single socks in their drawers and I was too busy to do much about it! But, I have found a clever little system that works great for us. I pulled every "single" sock out of all of the drawers in the house and put them into a reusable grocery bag. I then dumped them all on the floor and told the girls to come and see who could find the most matches. Whoever has the most wins...make a game of it! Now, when I have single socks during laundry time, I just throw them into my "sock bag" instead of into someone's drawer. This keeps the drawers neat, and every few months, we get to play the sock game again. Another bonus to this is that you always know where some single socks are to make sock puppets on those rainy or snowy days!

- Packing Lunches-get your kids involved in what goes into their lunches. They can fill water bottles, get bread out for sandwiches, etc.
- Cleaning the car-inside and out.

It is important to let your children know how much work it takes to run a household, and that they are a very important piece of the team that helps with all that work. Teach them to appreciate having clean clothes, a tidy home, and a healthy, home-cooked meal, and also the amount of effort that has to be extended to get those things.

Having a solid team on the home front is an excellent way to reduce your mom stress, and add a little more *you* time to your day, so don't delay in getting your team working for you.

On a nice hot day, let your kids go wild cleaning your vehicle. Soapy, wet sponges and hoses make for a clean car and a bunch of happy (and wet) kids. "Just find the game, and snap the job is done..."Mary Poppins

Responsibilities

Everyone in your family has responsibilities. Everyone has a role, a job, and should feel good about it. You are a part of something bigger! Help your kids feel good about being part of a team.

Reward Chart: Reward your children for their responsibilities. I have used a few different reward charts in the past, some homemade and some purchased. Try this homemade reward chart!

1. Take any sheet of paper of any size.
2. Use a ruler to divide the page into squares. I used to think of it like a homemade calendar. Instead of drawing on lines, you can also print off a blank calendar with squares.
3. Have your child write their name at the top, or do it for them if they are too young. Have them help you decorate the reward chart, with coloring, stickers, glitter or whatever they like. It is important that they are excited about this!
4. You decide what they get rewarded for. (Good listening, going on the potty, not sucking their thumb, clearing their plate, sharing, practicing music lessons, doing their homework, doing their chores, being respectful).
5. Decide how you want the chart to work (if they fill the whole thing, they get X, or if they get a full row, they get X). The

If you are eager to get started rewarding your children for good behavior, keep it simple and create your own. Let your children help you decorate their chart anyway they like and get them to help you display it somewhere that they will see it and be able to reach it easily. Let them put their rewards on themselves. All you need is paper and a pen to get going with this!

important thing here is to make it appropriate for their age group, and to make the reward something they will be motivated by. Discuss the "Reward Rules" with your kids so everyone knows what to expect.

6. You can use cool stickers (the Dollar Stores are great for stickers!) as rewards, or you can use a stamp, or you can just color in a star, heart or smiley face. It won't really matter to your child, as long as they are receiving positive attention!

7. Be sure you speak to them each time you reward them and tell them why they are getting rewarded. "Great job sharing that toy with the baby today!" "Thank you for putting your plate in the kitchen without me asking...I really appreciate that!" I like to give out BONUS rewards when I see REALLY good behavior. If my children listen as soon as I ask, I will usually add a Bonus to their reward. ("Great job going to get your jammies on as soon as I asked. That is a bonus reward for you, so give yourself 2!)

8. Sometimes when your children fill up their reward chart to the point that they earn the bigger reward, you won't be able to give them the reward right away. For example, if you have agreed that when their whole chart is full, they will get to (go out for lunch with you or pick a movie to watch, or pick a toy out of a treasure chest, or go to the zoo, or get a new coloring book, or pick out a new story, go to the park with mommy, get $5 allowance...). When they fill up their chart, simply create a "coupon" redeemable for the specified reward, and post that coupon by their chart. Plan to fulfill their reward as soon as it is convenient for your family so that your child has something to look forward to. Make a big deal out of it.

We used to use the homemade reward system for years. Then one day I discovered the Melissa and Doug Magnetic Chart. I bought three and we decided to try it out.

It is really cool because it runs on a week to week basis, and it breaks down a whole list of "responsibilities" that you can

These are the reward charts we use now. The chart comes with a bunch of magnetic chores like "take out garbage", "Make your bed", "Get Dressed", so it is very easy to make a list of things you'd like to work on improving in your household. It is also easy to keep the chores age appropriate. As with anything, modify the use to suit your family's needs.

change up each week. I found that my kids were just a bit too young (or I was just too lazy and it wasn't working for us) to conform to using all of the different chore lists. Instead, we just use the "Show Respect" responsibility. My children have to fill up the whole chart before they see any larger reward. This is the one place where I would say I am not totally consistent, but I am very rewarding! When I see amazing behavior, or when I need them to do something, I use rewards! Trinity has become very good at bartering for rewards. When I ask her to vacuum, she always asks for extra rewards. I say "I'll give you 2." She says "make it 3". She is my daughter!

Reward charts are meant to be a fun and motivating experience and a way of encouraging the behaviors that you want in your home. You can use them with your teenagers also (though you may want to upgrade to a more teenage-friendly looking chart), and at that time you can really assign specific chores for each child and switch it up week to week. You can base their allowance on how they did on their chore charts for the week. Add "bonus" rewards when your teens complete their chores without complaining!

Now that you know what you want (Planet Do-it!) and you have some tools to help you schedule yourself (Efficiency is the Key), it's time to find out if you are making good use of the time you have. I love to make you work in this book, but don't worry, I will go easy on you! I am not here to judge you and I want you to become very conscious of the fact that no one else should be judging you either. You are even guilty of judging yourself, using preconceived notions of how things should be, rather than how you would like things to be. Let all judgment and criticism go, opening yourself to the possibilities of YOU. You have to live your life — your life is here to be enjoyed by you. So create what YOU want! If you've never allowed yourself to be honest about what you want, I am now giving you permission to be FREE to decide, free to choose, free to dream, free to do anything that feels great!

I want you to know that you can create your life and mold it into any shape you like. The only thing holding you back right now is you. Isn't that great? Isn't that amazing? YOU have all the power. Oh yeah…that's what I'm talking about! Control and power to be used for the good of you. I am not a total control freak…I swear! (Well ok, *perhaps* I am, but hey I like myself that way!)

So, let's assess what you've been doing with your time, and see how YOU feel about that? Together, we're going to focus you on things that are really fun, awesome and rewarding.

It's time to WORK IT, Mom!

CHAPTER 4

Work It Momma

· ·

"Mothers always find ways to fit in the work –
but then when you're working, you feel that you should be
spending time with your children and then when you're with
your children, you're thinking about working."
– Alice Hoffman

As I sit here in Starbucks writing this book while my youngest daughter is in preschool for a couple of hours, I know with absolute certainty that I AM THAT MOM! I have set a goal for myself for the release of this book and I feel an amazing sense of pressure that is making me stick to that goal. I have no one telling me that it has to be released at any time…I am in control of that as my own publisher. Exciting things are always coming up that pull my focus away from my book. A beautiful sunny day appears and suddenly it's plastic pool, sprinkler, ice tea and ice cream time with my kids. With the snow finally gone, my garden secretly calls me throughout the day…taunting me to come and spend more time with it! And to top it off, my sister just had her first baby yesterday! Talk about distractions of the best kind. Alas, I have a deadline. I have committed to myself and to my readers to get this book done by a certain time. I could so easily put it off and push back the deadline…what's the big deal? Well, it's a big deal to me! If I keep putting it off, it will never get done. So, if you are reading this book, I've succeeded! I finished it using the very methods that I am passing on to you in this book. Believe me when I tell you that it's not always easy and I am not perfect. When those sunny days steal me into the yard to hang with my kids or my garden, I have to give up some relax time at night to continue with my writing. The excitement that I feel about completing this project fuels me into action.

Thoughts produce actions. Actions produce results. What we want is results, but what we so often forget is that results require actions. We've got to work for those results.

W-O-R-K. It's literally a four-letter word…
Will
Opportunity
Really
Knock?

Just hearing the word can inflict panic in a lot of people, whether they realize it or not. Sunday night can be the most stressful night of the week as people are overcome with thoughts of getting up for work on Monday morning.

Defined, as per the *Merriam-Webster Dictionary*, work is:

An activity in which one exerts strength or faculties to do or perform something:

a: sustained physical or mental effort to overcome obstacles and achieve an objective or result
b: the labour, task, or duty that is one's accustomed means of livelihood
c: a specific task, duty, function, or assignment often being a part or phase of some larger activity.

Work is perhaps best thought of as a simple exchange. We provide effort or time, and in exchange we are given something that has a perceived value. On the other end of the spectrum, there is retirement. The concept of retirement evokes images of sunny, palm tree-lined beaches and serene lakefront cabins with wraparound porches. Reading books, traveling the world, skiing and golfing. Doing all the things you could be doing right now if it wasn't for WORK.

Defined as per *Merriam-Webster*, retirement is:

> Withdrawal from one's position or occupation
> or from active working life.

The way we define retirement is to stop the exchange of effort that was getting us the desired results. But do we really want the results to stop? And, are we really prepared to stop putting effort into our lives, just to be retired? I certainly am not!

I now know with all of my heart that I have full control over my time. (So do you!) Getting to this point in my own head was not easy for me; I am a very committed person. When I say I am going to do something, I do it! I care deeply about not letting myself down. I always knew that I wanted to own my own business…my mom and dad instilled the entrepreneurial spirit in me at a very young age. My parents were also extremely supportive, optimistic, and they consistently told all of us kids that we could do anything we wanted.

Our first business was a liquor store; we bought it using the equity in our home. Once we had one store, Ryan and I put a plan into place that involved us owning and operating 5 stores. We ended up buying a second store and continued our search for our third, fourth and fifth stores. I loved having a goal that both Ryan and I could visualize in our lives and work towards. The stores became my little empire, while Ryan had his career working as an executive at a wireless company. For awhile, it was glorious. Then, something changed for me. The liquor store business was no longer giving me the rewards that I wanted and I longed to spend more time with my children. What was I to do? We had a plan. How could that be changed? I am not the kind of person that gives up.

The hardest thing for me was letting go of one path in my search for something better. I think it is extremely important to know that though you may be walking down one path right now, other paths will come along and you will define yourself by which path you take. I no longer believe that you need to stay on a pathway just because that is what you have always done, or that it was your plan before. Things change! You change! That is completely how life is supposed to be.

For over a year, I tried to find ways to keep the liquor store businesses going, while I freed up time to spend with my family or for pursuing my authoress adventures. Why couldn't I do it all? I did not want to give up on our original plan... it made me feel horrible. It made me feel like I was not being accountable to myself, or to Ryan and our goals. Over that year, I went through an intense grieving process. The liquor stores were my babies... my first babies! I had nurtured them and put all of my energy into those fantastic businesses; I had an amazing staff that I knew I would miss, and I could not see myself not having them. I had been defining myself based on what I did for work — I was an entrepreneur growing a chain of stores. Would I be the same if I sold them? Keeping the stores was frustrating, stressful, and emotionally draining on myself and my family. It took over a year for Ryan and I to actually make a solid decision to sell our business. Once the decision to sell the stores was made, things seemed to happen rather quickly. (Though still not quickly enough for me!)

Ryan and I created a new plan for ourselves that did not include the stores and suddenly I could taste the freedom! I realized that "giving up" something was required in order to allow the flow of other wonderful things into my life. Even me, the goddess of change, was afraid of letting go! Let me tell you, once my mind was made up, a whirlwind of interesting things started happening. It's all in your thinking... let me assure you! You are your own worst enemy when it comes to your life, but you can also be your own best friend if you choose to.

If something is not working for you, you have got to change something. Just because you've always done something does not mean you should keep doing it. It's perfectly ok to take a leap of faith and make a change in your life. In fact, allowing yourself to be redefined in your own mind and start walking down a different path will set you apart from others.

So... how will you know if you are walking the right path? The path you are on now may have started off smooth and easy, but you may be finding it harder and harder to walk along it. Weeds have started to block your view, large rocks have fallen, and are making it hard to keep moving forward. Perhaps a brick wall has been built right in front of you, or a bear has started chasing you back down the path from whence you came! It's OK to jump off your current path when you need to, or when you feel that it is the right time.

Trust me when I tell you that thinking about doing something is always scarier than actually just doing it.

I'd like to give you a real life example. We had sold our stores and were awaiting the possession date. Unfortunately, the new owners refused to take over our existing staff, so all of my amazing employees were going to be laid off. These wonderful people had worked hard for our business and while I realized that it was just business, I was sick to my stomach thinking about how I would tell my staff that in a few short weeks they would be without a job. It was bittersweet... I was getting exactly what I wanted, but my decision was definitely going to impact others. I would lay awake at night with sweaty palms pondering what I was going to say, visualizing what they would say to me and trying not to feel like a horrible person. Finally, I just had to stop thinking about it and do it! Shaky, sweaty and nervous, but maintaining my composure, I just did it and told them. Yes, it was bad, and yes they were upset, but it certainly was not as bad as what I was making it out to be in my own head. We have the ability to create extreme visions in our heads of the unknown, causing terrible fear and anxiety about things that may or may not even happen. Control yourself and do your best not to think too much! JUST DO IT! Don't let fear hold you back, or you will be stuck behind that brick wall for the rest of your life. Smash down the wall with all your strength and enjoy the feeling of being on the other side. Remember, if it was easy, everyone would be doing it. Get the courage, the strength and the DESIRE to change your direction and start enjoying your life more.

How you choose to spend your time will have a direct impact on the results you see in your life. I have created a simple exercise to help you assess your pathways. Is it time for a trim, or is it time to jump over to another path entirely?

Wouldn't it be nice if you could define your W-O-R-K as...

Welcoming

Opportunities

Revealing

Knowledge

It's time for another exercise! Get out 2 fresh sheets of paper and your favorite pen. At the top of one sheet, write "My Efforts". Write out the following 4 headings, leaving several blank lines after each one.

1. **Personal**
   a.
   b.
   c.
2. **Family**
3. **Home**
4. **Monetary**

Now I want you to write down everything you do to fill your time in a given month. You should be able to categorize your efforts under one of the headings listed above.

Below is an example of "My Efforts" to get you going.

1. **Personal**
   a. Getting myself ready to face the day. (meditation, showering, hair, makeup, teeth-brushing, creaming, etc.).
   b. Having lunch each week with my mom and sister.
   c. Dates with my husband, at home or going out.
   d. Hanging out with my friends.
   e. Doing Yoga.
   f. Reading.
   g. Watching TV.
   h. Getting at least 8 hours of sleep per day.

2. **Family**
   a. Getting my children ready for the day.
   b. Feeding my family breakfast and dinner.
   c. Making lunches for everyone to take to school, (done the day before to make mornings easier).
   d. Planning and scheduling the week for my family and myself.
   e. Driving my children to and from school and organizing play dates with their friends.
   f. Doing homework with my children.
   g. Volunteering at school for each of my three children's classes.
   h. Grocery shopping.
   i. Organizing family functions, like brunches, birthday parties and dinners.
   j. Organizing and driving my children to their extra curricular activities (swimming, music, hockey, figure skating, soccer, dance, etc.).

3. **Home**
   a. Making the beds everyday (currently, I make everyone's, although I am teaching my children the value of doing things for themselves as they get older). Opening up all of the blinds in the morning. I LOVE the act of "drawing the drapes" each day!
   b. Tidying and cleaning the house.
   c. Laundry.
   d. Watering plants.
   e. Gardening.
   f. Raking leaves, shoveling snow, property maintenance.
   g. Organizing and clutter maintenance.
   h. Compiling and managing the garbage and recycling on a weekly basis.

4. **Monetary**
   a. Networking- Going to events and finding other like-minded people to work with.
   b. Writing books!
   c. Promotional activities for the book business...book signings, TV appearances, events.
   d. Growing the book business. Securing distribution and publishing other author's titles.
   e. Communicating with lawyers and accountants about issues related to our businesses.
   f. Meeting with my incredible Manager, who is truly in charge of EVERYTHING.
   h. Social Media postings.
   i. Blog Postings.
   j. Website maintenance.
   k. Budgeting for both home and business, as well as banking.
   l. Further Education. (I am currently studying to become a Certified Feng Shui Practitioner...my absolute passion).
   m. I donate money and time to support amazing causes and help girls all around the world have access to MORE.

Write down at least 2 things you do under each category if you can. Your list will likely be very different than mine, and that is perfect! Be honest about how you spend your time. You may need to observe yourself for a week before completing this exercise, and make notes of what you do during the day in your journal. Or, if you are using an agenda as I suggest in the previous chapter, after a week you will have a pretty good idea of how you spend your time.

Now- it's time to assess your results! On the second piece of paper, write "My Results" at the top of the page. Write the same 4 headings that you used on your efforts page, making sure you leave several blank spaces between each one.

1. **Personal**
    a.
    b.
    c.

1. **Family**
2. **Home**
3. **Monetary**

For each line item on your efforts page, I want you to consider what result(s) you are getting, and then write them down. You do not need to come up with a result for every effort that you listed above. Often, our efforts will combine to produce a desired, or undesired, result.

Below is an example of some the Results I get in my life:

1. **Personal**
    a. I get noticed!
    b. I feel energetic and happy.
    c. I am in good physical shape.
    d. I have strong, close bonds with my family and friends.
    e. I am prepared, organized and (mostly) calm.

2. **Family**

    a. I have happy and healthy children who get what they need: love, attention, food, clothing, etc.

    b. Our family is not rushed in the morning. We all have a hearty breakfast together and everyone gets out of the house on time, feeling ready to take on the day. Everyone leaves the house with a prepared lunch. This saves time and money, and ensures that everyone eats something healthy.

3. **Home**

    a. I feel relaxed about the state of my home. Having things neat and tidy gives me a sense of order and allows me to focus on the tasks of the day.

    b. We all have clean clothes.

    c. My plants create cleaner air and add positive energy.

    d. Our home looks good, feels good, is positive, and allows for life-giving energy to flow into our lives every day.

4. **Monetary**

    a. The book publishing business provides me with the flexibility to be home with my children and still enjoy the rewards of running my own business. (You may choose to write down how much money you receive in exchange for your efforts).

    b. I am learning every day how to be better at everything.

    c. I inspire people (including myself) every day.

    d. I generate enough money to suit the lifestyle that I want.

    e. I am able to donate a portion of my time and money to an amazing cause...I love being able to help others in this way.

Now, look over both of your lists and take some time to ponder the following questions in your mind. If you still have space on your worksheets, take a moment to write down your answers. You may also choose to write the questions and the answers in your journal, or notebook, since you now have one on you all the time...right? You know now how powerful writing things down can be!

Here are your questions:

- How do you feel about how you are spending your time?
- Are you balancing your time well across all categories, or is your time being focused largely on one category?
- Are you getting the results you want in each category? Is there room for improvement?
- Do you feel that the exchange you make in time is worth what you are receiving? Do you feel like you are giving up more than you are receiving?

You are your own boss in this life. You are in charge of the results that you see and that is a huge responsibility! That being said, you are the only one that can be held responsible for where you are right now. As Trooper would sing "If you don't like what you got, why don't you change it?"

If you are not happy with some, or all of your current results, you have two choices:

1. Do something differently.
2. Change the way you think.

No matter what you decide to do, you must be prepared to put in the effort and take action in your life. You must do the work, put in the time, learn more and strive for more.

Changing what you do can be simple or hard. It can be something small, or something big. It can be exciting, or it can be stressful. Often, the difference is a matter of your own perception. Get excited about change, as it is the only thing in this life that is inevitable. Standing still and taking no action will end in little or no positive results. Always take action.

Remember too that **being busy does not equal being successful**. You do not need to justify your existence by being busy all the time. A big part of being 'That Mom' is learning to distinguish between being successful and being a control freak.

If the work you are doing to earn money currently is not satisfying you, it's time to change it! If you are not happy with the way your home is functioning, perhaps you and your partner need to put more effort into your home. I cannot stress to you enough that this is a personal exercise. Only you will know if you are pleased with the results and only you will be able to change it. There are only so many hours in a day, so shift things around to create more fulfillment in all of the areas of your life starting now!

Ask yourself, "how can I make things better in my life?" Remember that you only have two options; create tangible change in your life, or create change in your thoughts. If you have decided to change something in your life, you must also give yourself the power to feel excited about this change. You know that you want to change something. You have decided to proceed. You have taken the biggest step to success. You've made a decision, now stick to it!

Be accountable to yourself. Get excited about your own power. Take the control back. And never, ever, let fear stand in the way of your dreams again. The amazing things you dream for your life cannot be obtained unless you stay focused and start taking action to achieve those goals. Get into the groove of embracing change. Once you convince yourself to embrace change, you will find yourself more excited about what each day will bring.

If you decide not to change what you are doing, you have only one other choice - change your thinking. Stop complaining about being unhappy with the results in your life. You have the power to change those results and you have chosen not to, so you must actually be happy with what you have. Imagine that! *"You got to ac-cent-tu-ate the positive and e-lim-i-nate the negative…"* Harold Arlen and Johnny Mercer sure knew what they were talking about. Instead of complaining and feeling unhappy about things, do this instead: Every morning when you wake up, think of one amazing thing about your life and write it down. You should still have your journal on the go, so just use that. No need to date anything or write any more than a sentence.

Think of something new every day. Balance your thinking to include amazing things from all the different areas of your life as the weeks progress.

Here are some examples to get you thinking, and writing!

Relationships

My daughter told me she appreciates me today...and she took her own plate in without me asking! (Celebrate life's little moments!)

Efforts (Work, School, Volunteering)

I love volunteering weekly at my child's school, and I was able to drop everything and head to school when I was needed for a meeting. (Can you believe that my kids were spreading around the Bloody Mary story and were freaking out all of the younger kids? Wait, my kids are perfect...that must have been someone else's kids!)

Home

I love our house, even though the roof has been leaking . I will take pride in my home and prioritize fixing it this year!

Results (Paycheck, Free Time, Vacation, Things)

I volunteer at my children's school and take three weeks of vacation every year without hassle. I may not make a lot of money, but the time I have is worth its weight in gold.

Health

I feel energized and I rarely get sick for more than a day.

Self

I sat and had a coffee by myself today and read my book for a half an hour.

Try to do this every day and keep it going forever. Even when things get you down, there is always one thing in your life that is positive. Remember the positive things and focus on them. The human mind can only hold one thought at a time so make it a good one!

Do not worry or complain. You will create whatever you think about in your life, so what have you been creating lately? Are you satisfied? Start creating new results if you're not. It's simple.

Two choices. Door number one: do something different. Or door number two: change the way you think. Remember, you are the one in control. Take the reins and let happiness start pouring into your life every day. It's all a matter of perspective and actions.

What we strive for is to get great results from our actions. Communicating effectively, with yourself, your family, your co-workers or bosses, is an important way to ensure you get the results you want...so let's chat!

CHAPTER 5

Communication

· · · · · · · · · · · · · · · · · · · ·

Time to Talk

"Communication breakdown, it's always the same"
– Led Zeppelin

Whenever you have a family, or any group of people living together under the same roof for that matter, there are bound to be interesting dynamics. Each person has their own unique personality, their own goals, their own thoughts and feelings, and yet all must learn to live as a cohesive family unit, supporting each other and respecting each other's desires, while also respecting common goals.

Building a solid team requires solid communication, something that does not always come easily. As you watch your children go through emotions, it will inevitably take you back to being a child and how frustrating it was when someone did not understand you, for whatever reason. I believe everyone struggles with the frustration of trying to get our point across and our message understood properly at every age. That is the essence of communication. Learning to communicate better as a family is a gift that will carry you all through this amazing journey called life.

Growing up, I was never very good at expressing my feelings. I could identify that I was feeling something intense — sometimes it was good, and sometimes it was bad — but I didn't know how to put those emotions into words. I struggled when it came to interacting with others; I would use a reactive behavior rather than talk about my feelings. Often, once I figured out what was setting me off, it turned out to be a misunderstanding, or just a fabricated worry in my own head. Now that I am a mom, I can appreciate the value of working through emotions and really working on feeling great all the time. We can all learn to be even better communicators while we help our children learn the tools they need to thrive.

Involve your children in what is happening in your life. It affects them to, and they should be kept in the loop. Time for a family meeting! Whether you are moving, having money trouble, having relationship issues, switching careers or anything else that impacts your life, discuss it as a family at an age appropriate level. The more open you are in discussing your feelings and situations, the more your children will learn to share everything with you. That is what we want and need as moms! We want our kids to talk to us, to trust us, and to keep us in their circle of confidence. "Knowing is half the battle" –GI Joe!

Plus, you never know what kind of ideas your children will have to contribute to your discussions. They are people too, and they have opinions that need to be heard. Communication is key in every relationship, but especially between moms and their children. Most disagreements are the result of poor communication issues or inconsistencies in communication, where the parties communicating do not understand where the other person is coming from, and vice versa. This happens constantly with my three daughters (girl power.... RRROWR!) Someone's feelings get hurt and the other doesn't take notice or seem to care. Next thing you know there are tears, then yelling, then either an all-out hair-pulling *battle royale* or someone sulking alone in their room.

It's never going to be easy to communicate with kids, but it can be easier if you work at it and start before they can even talk.

Communicating with Babies — Hanging around with a bunch of new moms is awesome! Everyone has new products, or information to share with each other and I always found it a great way to stay "up" on things. When I had Trinity, one of my new-mom friends ended up hosting a "baby sign" class at her house. I was intrigued and made a point of going. This was something that I had long been interested in, ever since I made it a priority of mine when I was younger to learn the ABC's in sign language.

It was fascinating to learn that Baby Sign Language is an extremely effective way of communicating with your children before they can even talk. It is a legitimate language that uses parts of the brain that are different from those that you use for spoken or written words. By using Baby Sign Language, you are actually teaching your baby a new language. I knew right away that it was something I wanted to pursue with my baby.

Trinity was just a few months old when we took the class, and we were introduced to the DVD series *Signing Time* (signingtime. com). I fell in love with *Signing Time* right from the start. The DVDs are made for kids — the signs are shown fairly slowly, then paired with fun, catchy music. The signs featured are for very basic things that you would actually use everyday with your children: concepts like milk, cookies and play (a few of my own personal favorites).

These DVD's will have you singing with your kids in no time. Learn a new language and you'll have a fun new way of communicating with your family!

When Trinity was a baby, I would watch the DVDs mostly by myself (I hadn't yet started using the TV as a babysitter with Trinity) and then use what I learned on a daily basis, even while Trinity was just a few months old. When I would nurse her, I would say: "you're having milk, Trinity, milk…" and I would do the sign for "milk." I found it so easy to learn the signs and I was excited about the idea of using a "new language" and interested to see how my baby would respond.

It was incredible; I am not going to lie. At around four or five months, Trinity started signing "milk" and "eat." It didn't stop there. Not surprisingly, "more" was a sign that all my kids commonly used.

What I found especially interesting was how easily my daughter was able to "talk" to me, without actually using her vocal cords. She could ask for what she wanted, say "no," say "yes," let me know which foods she liked, whether she wanted water or milk, and if she was "all done." She also knew how to understand and sign her emotions. How interesting is it to be able to teach your child about a feeling before they are one year old and have them be able to express the fact that they are tired, sad, happy, scared or excited? When you teach sign language to babies, you are actually helping them learn our vocabulary before the physical parts of speech have fully developed. You may even notice that your "signing" baby speaks more clearly and with a larger vocabulary, once they do begin talking (though this isn't something that happens with every child).

Practicing sign language with your child at any age requires effort on your part, as you have to learn the signs yourself; however, the reward is that the communication between you and your children will improve. Sometimes our children don't have, or can't get out, the words they need to express how they feel, or what they need. But giving them the power of sign language provides them with another tool they can use to get their "words" out, hopefully reducing those inevitable communication-related meltdowns. Watch the *Signing Times* DVDs together as a family. You will be amazed at how quickly and easily you can pick up the signs and your family will be singing the tunes and doing the actions in no time.

I found that we used signs a lot with our children until they had a really good grasp on spoken language and then we sort of just stopped, although we still pull out certain signs if we need to communicate with each other in a packed room, and we still sign "I love you" to each other every day and night.

The Big D (Discipline) — One of the most important things when it comes to dealing with your kids is to be consistent. If you say you are going to do something, you need to do it. This develops a trust relationship between you and your kids. They will know that if you say they have "five more minutes," you literally mean five more minutes.

This applies in all kinds of situations. Being consistent will reduce outbursts and temper tantrums because your children will know that when you say something, you mean it. When you say "no!" to them asking you to buy them candy at the grocery store, then they will not to ask you 20 more times after that. "No" literally means "no."

If you give in to them after you have already said "no," trust me, they will remember and they will push you to your limit (and beyond) in the future. Kids are extremely savvy this way and they are innately motivated to get what they want. So be careful how you answer their questions in the first place. Do not be wishy-washy. You are the mom! Stand your ground no matter how hard they grind you. It will pay off.

Of course, if they continue to misbehave, or refuse to listen to you, there needs to be a consequence. Certain disciplinary techniques are more effective than others. Disciplining your kids isn't about hurting them, but about behaviour modification — teaching them that what they did was not ok and that they shouldn't do that again in the future. The goal of any sort of discipline is to help your children learn what is appropriate and what is not appropriate, and to help them learn how to be great listeners. Children often do not understand that they need to listen to their parents for their own safety. We are not just being control freaks! (Well, most of the time, we're not).

I've found the "time out" system to be a very effective technique with all of my girls. A time out can also be thought of as "thinking time." It is a chance for everyone to take a break so they can assess and think about the situation at hand. I find that a time out can really reduce the emotion level for everyone — time heals, the saying goes.

Select a spot in your home that will work for a time out. The space should be somewhere accessible and close to the part of the house where you spend most of your time. The place that you assign for time outs in your home should remain consistent. You may choose to use a stair for them to sit on, a "special" chair that stays in one spot, a mat, or even just a certain space on the carpet or floor. The point here is to have a spot that is designated for "time outs." When there is an issue that you feel warrants a time out (you get to decide what those things are), you will calmly tell your child that they have earned a time out.

The countdown method is another way to encourage changes in behaviour. My cousin Julie used this method with her kids, which she pulled from the parenting book *1-2-3 Magic* by Thomas W. Phelan, PhD. Give your child fair warning that if they do not shift their behavior, they will be given a time out. Then say, "that's one." Behaviour still not where you want it? You say "that's two," and if that doesn't work, then you tell them "That's three. You've earned a timeout."

However you get to that point, when you deem that a time out is to be given, place your child directly in the time out space (stair, chair, mat, etc) and tell them how long they will be there. A good way to gauge how long to make a time out is to use the child's

age: a three-year-old gets three minutes; a five-year-old five minutes, and so on. Use a timing device to keep track. For the sake of
consistency, I've found it's best to use the same timer, as they will
learn quickly what their "done" time sounds like. Do not speak
with the child during their time out. The time out is an opportunity for them to think about the situation that got them there and
for everyone's emotions to settle. If you are having trouble getting
your child to stay on the time out, try not to look at them or talk
to them, just continue to place them back at the spot where they
have been told they need to stay.

Once again, it is crucial that you *be consistent*! Decide how you
will handle disobedience with the time out and stick to that plan.
My kids serve their time outs on the stairs. If I give my children a
time out and they do not go to the stairs themselves (I have to chase
them or they just decide not to go there, or they are yelling at me), I
start adding minutes to their time out and I stick by it. I have trained
them to go and sit for their time outs by themselves and that if they
sit quietly for the entire time they know that their "thinking time"
will be over in the shortest amount of time. Kids do not enjoy time
outs, so they do not appreciate having them get longer.

I also add minutes to the time out if they scream at me or
talk back while they are sitting on the stairs. If they are hollering,
throwing things, kicking, or displaying other bad behaviours on
their time out, calmly let them know that they have just earned an
extra minute (or two or four...whatever you feel is appropriate).
Not that my kids ever do things like that...

Once the time out is done, it is important to discuss with your
child why they were given a time out. What we really want is for
them to learn from the disciplinary process so it's important not
to skip this step. Ask them if they remember why they were put on
a time out and give them a chance to respond to you. Do not be
surprised if they cannot tell you why. Then explain to them what
happened (you spit your food all over the table for no reason,
you threw your ball at the kitchen window, you ripped the ear off

your sister's teddy bear). Let them know how it made you feel, or how it would have made the other affected people feel. Use descriptive words for emotions. Ask why they did the improper behavior and give them a chance to talk about their feelings. Help them describe their feelings. "Were you angry at your sister for not playing with you? Did that make you feel sad, or upset, or frustrated?" It is important to give children options for words to describe their feelings. Talking things over can really help both you and your child understand each other better (and understand the world better).

It is not easy to describe a feeling, even for adults. Communicating with your child and letting them know that you understand them is extremely important. Tell them you love them no matter what and help them figure out better ways of handling frustrating situations. Always encourage your children to use their words instead of their actions to express themselves. This is why it is so important to give your children lots of choices for words to use to express themselves. Getting the emotions out in a constructive way through words (or signs) helps your children build lasting relationships as they go forward in their lives. Give your child the time and the resources they need to thrive on their own. It is well worth the extra time and effort and you will learn things about yourself along the way.

Be careful not to dish out negative attention to your child while they are on their time out. Once of my daughters loves to sit on the stairs and scream: "Mommy, I just need to talk to you!" If you keep responding to them while they are screaming at you, they will be happy to get the attention, no matter what kind of attention it is. Again, simply let them know that you will speak with them when they are done their time out and then leave it at that. Add time calmly, where necessary, to prevent and curtail improper behaviour.

If you are consistent, kids will soon figure out the routine. But as with many things, the training part can be hard on both of you.

Remember that other adults and authority figures in your home also need to know your time-out rules and procedures. Babysitters, grandparents, aunts and uncles — anyone who is around your child needs to abide by the same routine. It is most important to have your partner follow the same guidelines as inconsistencies between parents can really cause problems.

Do not give kids a "next time you do that" warning. If a time out-worthy offense happens in your home, you need to address it then and there, not the "next time" that behavior happens. It is important for your child to realize that if they do something that is not appropriate or dangerous there will be a consequence right away. So, naughty behavior equals time out. Second chances will cause you twice as many problems down the road.

One mistake that parents often make (I still catch myself doing this) is to give their child directions in the form of a question. For example: "Payton, do you want to go get dressed now?" when what you really mean is: "Payton, go and get dressed now please." Be direct in your directions! If you ask your kids a question, they are bound to answer you, and it's almost a guarantee that "NO!" will be the answer. Be sure that your children know what their responsibilities are in the home. They should follow your directions if you are consistent. Be sure to thank them and praise them when they do what you ask them to do (especially if they do it the first time you ask).

Ripping Off the Band-Aid — When it comes to kids, in certain situations it's best to "rip off the Band-Aid" quickly rather than drag things out. Of course, I'm not referring to an actual Band-Aid, but to taking care of a situation with a quick, decisive motion that may cause immediate discomfort, though that discomfort will dissipate quickly in the aftermath. The other word for this philosophy is "cold turkey" and it can be employed in the following kid situations:

- **Taking away a soother**

  In my opinion, this is bound to be harder on you than it is on the child. You have to be the strong one! Do not allow yourself to be swayed by your child's emotions. You are likely to feel worse about it than they do. If you are ready to take it away, just do it. Attempting to "ease" them out of it will just breed confusion: "So, I can have it sometimes, but not other times? Only at bedtime, but not in the day? Wait, you just gave me my soother in the day because I was crying! I want it all the time!" If you remove the stimulus entirely your child will start to understand that it is no longer a part of their routine. Again, realize that this will be harder on you. You may have to deal with a little more crying than you are used to, but eventually, everything will adjust to normal.

- **Taking away the bottle**

  Again, when it comes to baby bottles, it's best to go "cold turkey." Say bye-bye to *all* of the bottles and remove them completely from your home (unless you'll need them again, in which case, hide them really, really well!) They will soon forget about their "baa baas." Trust me. As a mom, you will probably worry they are not getting enough milk without their daily or nightly bottles, but there are ways that you can help bridge this gap. Buy a few cool new cups that you know your child will like. Once the bottles are gone, just serve them their milk in the new cups. They will soon realize that the bottles aren't coming back and eventually drink their milk, as expected, out of their cups, just like the rest of their family. This will become their new "normal." Avoid saying things like: "Oh, you must miss your bottles, you're not drinking your milk anymore!" Just make it as unremarkable as possible that your child is transition-ing to a cup. They can sense your stressed-out energy and your worry. The less negative you are and the more normal you make a situation for your child, the easier it will be for them to handle. Give them attention in other positive ways and reward them for reaching a new stage in their lives "Wow, we are so proud of you! Look at you drinking out of that cool, big-girl cup!"

- **Leaving them with others-Caregivers, School, etc.**

  Your children will go through phases where they are completely attached to you, and are afraid of being left with others. When you need to take your children to other places for their care, it can be hard on both you and your child. Your children will not always be happy when you choose to leave them with others, and they will make sure you know that they are no pleased. They may kick, cry, scream, hold your leg and pull at your clothes when you try to leave. You will be tempted to stay and hug your child for long periods of time while they cry about the fact that you are leaving. Rest assured, the longer you stay, the harder it is going to be on both of you. Your child will get more upset and your adrenaline will be pumping the whole time. If you are confident that the place you are taking your baby (day home, day care, grandparents, school, camp) is a safe environment with adults who will provide responsible care, then you should feel great about leaving your child there no matter how your child reacts. In these situations, you can use the rip the 'Band-Aid' off quick method. Take your child in the door, have your quick chat with your sub-in(s), kiss and hug your child and let them know you will be back soon, and you love them. Then walk out the door. Yes, you will hear them screaming as you run to your van. And I am not saying this is easy. But, your child will stop crying fairly quickly after you leave, and you will be reducing the amount of time that they would spend freaking out about you leaving when you haven't already left. Each time you pick your child up at the end of the day, you are building their confidence. Each time that you drop your child off somewhere, you must act like it is no big deal and your child will quickly realize that this is just normal. Don't feed into the behavior you don't want. Reward the behavior you do!

Each child is different and each child will need different things from you. Be aware of this and be sensitive to their needs. Consistent communication and lack of judgment on your part when your children communicate with you will help your children feel comfortable talking to you about anything, anytime. This is exactly what we are striving for as mothers!

You will find yourself wishing that each challenging phase your child goes through will be over: the dreaded "terrible twos," teething, potty training, sleeping through the night, the teenaged years. All of these phases will seem to go on forever while you're in them, but in the end, your children will grow up faster than you think. You will find yourself wondering how it all could have gone by so quickly. Make sure you appreciate them along the way. Take "time outs" for yourself and enjoy your life. It's okay to take breaks. You deserve them. You work hard and *you are amazing!*

As a mom of kids of any age, the best thing I can tell you is this: remember to breathe. When you find yourself smack in the middle of a frustrating situation, walk away, take three big, deep breaths, and then come back to it. Taking even a microscopic break will tame some of the big emotions that might get in the way of handling the situation in a calm and reasonable manner.

Our children do their very best every day. When things get rough, take a time out for yourself and have a cup of tea. Things can look very different once you have taken a step back, and assessed the situation without those supercharged emotions.

Guiding Right — Our job as parents is to guide our kids through their journey to independence. Yeah… that's right. One day, your kids will be *independent* of you. You may not like to think about this, but it is extremely important. Your job as a mother is to teach your children how to live on their own. It is your job to help your children get the skills they will need to survive *without you*.

Before my husband Ryan and I ever had children of our own, his sister Debra instilled in me this valuable fact. All too often I see moms who are overtly attached to their children and the children, likewise, are utterly attached to them. I am not judging here, but merely stating a fact. Of course we are going to bond with our children and be attached to them! However, I believe it's unhealthy to view your children as possessions rather than extensions of you, or students of life. We are their mentors and their teachers and we must teach them how to be successful in a world that is often unfair, difficult and scary.

As a mom, hopefully you will have supportive people in your life, whether it is your parents or a partner. If you are parenting with someone else (your child's father or a life partner), it is important to stick together and present a united front, even when you don't agree with each other. Do not allow your children the option of getting something different out of one parent /caregiver over the other, as this will set up animosity or untrusting feelings between you and your partner. Talk to each other about the situation later on, maybe once the kids are in bed for the night. The important thing is that you don't have this talk in front of them. Stick by each other's decisions in the kids' presence and communicate about your disagreements behind closed doors.

Truth and Consequences — Consequence is a great teacher. You want to be able to tell your children what to do because you have done it before, and you experienced the consequences of your actions, and because of that, you do not want your children to have to go through some of the things that you did. Help your children realize what a consequence is:

> **Action** = consequence
> **Specific action** = specific consequence

Resist the urge to raise your children in a protective bubble. Life involves risk-taking and good risks can equal great rewards. The key is to minimize bad risks and maximize good risks. Pay careful attention to the consequences that occur as a result of actions. Point these consequences out to your children when you see them and help them become more aware of watching for results. Help your children make judgments based on the rewards (outcomes) of each action. A positive reward or outcome will fuel more positive behavior.

Assist your children with assessing their results. For example: Do you see what happened when you just grabbed the toy away from your brother? Now your brother is crying, and Mommy is taking the toy away. Do you think there was a better way to get the toy? What else could you have done?

Give them an opportunity to think and answer your questions. Encourage them to communicate back to you. Then provide them with options: you could have brought a different toy over to your brother and traded him for the toy you wanted; you could have used your words and asked nicely for the toy; you could have asked mommy for help; you could have said something like: "Can I play with that toy when you are done, please?" Provide consequences for your children to help them make better choices in the future. Don't get mad- give consequences!

The same goes for older kids and teens. For example: "Thank you for calling me when you got a speeding ticket while you were out in the car today. I really appreciate you letting me know about that. Please make sure you slow down in the future and you are going to have to work some extra hours at your part-time job to pay that off on time." Versus: "I just found a speeding ticket in your jeans while I was doing your laundry today. Why didn't you tell us about that? Speeding tickets happen, but I need you to be up front and honest with me anytime something happens while you have our vehicle. You are grounded from the car for a month, so you are going to have to take the bus to your part-time job to work extra hours to pay for that ticket, which is now past the early-rate date and costs twice as much."

When your kids have done something they shouldn't, praise them for telling you the truth and don't freak out at them. Keep the lines of communication open at all times. You want them talking to you. Don't make it scary for them to come to you with their problems or issues or concerns. We moms need to keep our inclination to freak out to ourselves sometimes! Let it out with your husband/partner or a parent, friend, or supporter, but don't let your kids know your innermost opinions in the heat of the moment. Instead, make your child feel comfortable and help them learn from each situation. If there is too much emotion, especially negative, it will be very difficult for your child to take any guidance from you. Our role as mothers is to help our children learn to handle situations. Be the "good teacher," not the "bad cop."

You know you are doing something right when your daughter says to you, in all seriousness: "Mom, you know you can talk to us about anything, right?" On the surface, it's funny in a "kids say the darndest things" sort of way, but on a deeper level it's encouraging for kids to understand the importance of open communication. Do not underestimate their knowledge and awareness. They are smarter and more perceptive than you think. They want to help you out. Keep them involved as much as you can and always communicate with them!

Recently Ryan went downstairs to chill out and watch some TV and all three girls came to join him on the couch. He hit the power button and the TV came to life on a random channel that just happened to be playing a movie with adult themes. Realizing this, Ryan tried frantically to change the channel, but in the split second that it took him to do that, one of the characters from the movie was heard saying: "…she was just playing with her dildo." The damage was done. All of the girls were asking: "Daddy, what's a dildo?" Being the awesome parent that he is, Ryan used "the distraction technique" — in this case, he chose to ignore the question and instead changed the subject to the family movies that were playing that night. The point of this story is that you don't have to tell your kids everything! It is appropriate to answer certain questions when they are ready to process the information. You will know when they are ready. You will feel it!

When I was in Grade 2, we moved into a new house. My parents had a waterbed at the time, but since they hadn't filled it that first night at the new house, they ended up sleeping on the floor of the living room, which was close to my room. The next morning, I gathered my courage and went to my mom to ask her: "Mommy, it sounded like daddy was hurting you last night." My mom reassured me that daddy was not hurting her. A few days later she gave me two books: *Where did I come from?* and *What's Happening to Me?* Both used cartoon-like illustrations to explain all about the things my mom thought I was ready to know. I sat in my room and read the books on my own. Looking back, I am not sure that I was ready!

Recently, my youngest daughter Payton (age five) came to me and said: "Mom, I don't really want to tell you this, 'cause it's just too funny." To which I replied: "Oh, you can tell me Payton, go ahead." Giggling, Payton said: "Trinity (my eldest) told me that a boy puts his penis in a girl's vagina! Isn't that hilarious!" Keeping my cool, I replied: "Yes, that is true Payton, and that is how babies are made."

Inside, however, I was freaking out! Because of this exchange I found out that my nine-year-old has been talking about sex — to my five-year-old! Oh the joy of having older siblings! So I guess that means it's time for *Where did I come from?* and *What's happening to me?* Aaaaarrrrrrgggggghhhhh!

Seriously, though, it is OK to be up front with your kids. The less weird you make tough subjects like sex and the more you open up to them, the more you will build trust as they mature into teenagers and eventually into adults. Keep that communication going! Don't let it "break down." I so easily could have said something like: "Payton, do NOT talk about that! That is disgusting! I am going to talk to Trinity and give her a time out for talking to you about that!" And believe me, I was tempted to go that route. But what would that do for my relationship with Payton down the road?

Ryan and I have decided that when it comes to these sensitive subjects it's best to teach our children the proper names of things and how biologically our bodies work. From a purely scientific standpoint, we would much rather call something what it is, even if it is a hilarious word. Why are those words so hilarious to us... *penis, vagina, breasts?* If you make such words less "interesting" to your kids by using them properly and not laughing when you say them, your kids will just think they are normal words (which they are). You will have to instruct them on appropriate times for discussing these words, but that comes with age and socialization. If my kids ask me a question (about menstruation or something of the sort), I try to answer it age appropriately.

Likewise, you need to do what you think is right for your kids. Everyone will have their own ideas about what they want their kids to know at what age. Do try to remember that they will start hearing things at school and on TV and that you cannot shelter them forever. They will interpret what they hear based on what little information they already have. Again, communication is key. Do you want them to know the facts? The only way you will know what they are hearing is to communicate and ask questions. It's never too early to start a trust relationship with your kids. Try not to act shocked when they ask you about boyfriends or girlfriends, or sex, or anything else (drinking, drugs, etc.). Encourage communication and let them feel comfortable. Allow them to trust that they can talk to you about anything. If it feels weird to them, they won't bring it up again, so be careful how you react. The more "off-limits" and secretive we make things, the more attractive those things become to kids — they want to know about things and they will do just about anything to find out. With the advent of the Internet, access to information is at their fingertips. If you won't tell them, they'll find out anyway. If you talk to them, at least you'll know what they are learning, and you can have an impact on them by how you present the information.

Try to explain to your children the "why" of restricting them from things, rather than just saying no, or "you're not allowed." I hated it when my mom would just say "no!" without offering a reason. I actually started coming up with arguments as to why I should be able to do the things I had been restricted from doing as an attempt to persuade my mother to allow me to do those things. I wanted a good reason for "no!"

Growing up, I had friends who were allowed to do just about anything. They could eat what they wanted, go where they wanted — they had "total freedom." I felt so restricted, held down by so many rules. What I realize now is that my parents cared so deeply for me that they put those rules in place to keep me safe and keep me healthy.

Now, when I talk to my kids, I make sure I tell them why that rule is there. They may not understand, and if they do, they still might not agree, but at least I have said my piece and provided them with a reason. I often say: "I love you too much to let you do that (jump off the dressers onto the bed, run across the road without looking, eat junk food all the time). They will thank you one day, even if you feel like a nag now.

Encourage your children to write their feelings down. Every child is sensitive in their own way and encouraging them to keep a diary or journal, and write to themselves (or to God, or the Universe), is an amazing way to help them start assessing and recognizing their feelings and putting words to them. In the beginning, ask them to share the journal with you just so you can guide them in the process of putting things down on paper. Even drawing pictures can be an outlet for a child's feelings. As they get older, make it known to everyone in the house that journals are personal and are not to be read without permission. Make it a big deal that everyone respects the privacy of others. This will build trust amongst everyone in the home.

When my children have problems at school with someone, I encourage them to write a letter to that person (the letter may or may not get delivered). Have them use phrases like: "You made me really sad, angry, upset, frustrated, left out when you did that specific action." Expressing yourself can be difficult, so help your children with the words in the beginning. They need to be able to associate a feeling with a word.

I also encourage my children to speak their feelings to their friends and classmates when there is a conflict or disagreement. "Use your words!" is something I tend to say on a regular basis. When my middle daughter was being bullied at school by one of her classmates, I thanked her for telling me about it and then gave her some strategies to address the situation the next time she came face to face with the other student. I helped her practice what she would say and then we talked about what might happen next and how to handle it. What we came up with was: "You better leave me alone. I told my mom that you are treating me this way so she knows about it. If you don't stop, I am going to tell the teacher!"

Even though we can't be with our kids all the time, we can give them the tools they need to get through a difficult situation. If your child suddenly starts acting differently in any way, it's usually a sign something is bugging them. Encourage communication —with you, with their friends, with their teachers, with everyone! Role-playing will help them come up with phrases that might be useful in the various situations they might encounter.

This will give them the confidence and self esteem they need to help themselves. Confidence and good self-esteem will help your child handle any situation.

Encourage communication at the dinner table. Have each family member say one thing that happened to him or her that day. Everyone else must be quiet and listen to the person talking, and after that person is done, others can comment, or ask questions. Do this with your spouse or partner also, and have your kids also ask you about your day. You will find your children telling you the good, the bad and the ugly at the dinner table. It's a great place to share your thoughts and feelings, together as a family. You will all learn a lot about each other. Younger siblings will have an opportunity to hear how people express themselves, and everyone will learn to listen and communicate with each other better. Make dinner time a chance to reconnect with each other. You care deeply for your family, and caring enough about them to ask about their day will show them how much you value them and the things that happen with them.

Be sure to take the time to give your children your undivided attention. When they talk to you, make sure you make eye contact with them. Ask them to do the same when you are talking to them, especially if you are having a serious discussion. I find my children always want to look away from me when I am talking to them about a negative behaviour or a situation in which they acted inappropriately (yep, they're getting in trouble). I always ask them to look at me when I talk to them. Eye contact is an important part of communication and they deserve to have your undivided attention when you are talking them just as much as you deserve to have theirs.

Children must also learn to be patient. They often demand your attention when you are right in the middle of an important phone call or conversation. If you are on the phone, this is where knowing a little sign language will come in handy. Teach your children to be respectful of you and of your time. They will need to wait at times for you to address their concerns. Be sure to thank them for waiting once you are done and then give them your undivided attention. If they scream and holler for your attention, be sure to let them know (as calmly as you can) that that is not an appropriate way of handling themselves (perhaps a time out might be called for in that situation). We all want attention, and none of us likes to wait (least of all me!) but we do need to learn to be respectful to each other. That's one of the best things your kids can learn as they grow up and prepare to take on the world.

Taking on the world is a pretty big task for anyone and it requires you to be healthy, vibrant, strong and well rested if you are going to succeed. Here are a few simple ways for you to help your family exude health so you can take on the world together!

Be That
MOM™

· ·

*"Always be prepared to listen WHENEVER
they want to talk about something... no matter
what time of day. DO NOT say, 'it's late let's
talk about this tomorrow,' as you may not get
a second chance. My daughter did her best
unloading at two in the morning and
that kept her from dropping out of school."*

— *Cari Middleton*

· ·

CHAPTER 6

Family Health

. . . .

Eat Well, Feel Well

"Let food be thy medicine and medicine be thy food."
– Hippocrates

Keeping your family healthy is one of the most important parts of being "That Mom", but it's also one of the toughest things to do! If only we could cover each child with padding and a helmet and a mask — on second thought, make that two masks, one to protect their teeth and one to stop the contamination of germs. Then all we'd have to do is figure out some way to control what they put in their mouths, and it would be so much easier to keep everyone healthy. On top of all this, we need to keep ourselves healthy, too.

I believe that when you start having kids, you really start to evaluate what you are doing to your own body. You see the sweet, fragile, perfect bodies that your children are born with and you dedicate your energy toward helping your child keep that body healthy and vibrant. It makes you think about what you are doing to your own body. If you wouldn't let your child have something, why would it be OK for you? (Of course, there are exceptions to every rule. Wine, for instance…)

The point is, as moms, we too have beautiful, strong bodies and we need to care for those bodies. If we give our bodies what they need, we will have no problem warding off sickness and exuding health, energy and vitality. There will always be germs. You need to prepare yourself and your family to fight these germs by adding the armor of a healthy immune system. Some people just never get sick. They are not superheroes with incredible powers, they just have incredible immune systems; super-human shields that never allow any germy badness to override their systems.

In my opinion, here are the ingredients for a healthy family:

- Healthy diet
- Clean water
- Sleep
- Natural health remedies
- Shelter
- Fun (this can also be considered exercise)
- Sunshine and fresh air (a.k.a. outdoor exercise)
- Love

That's it! I'm serious. I know this list is pretty small. There are also a lot of things that we think we need to have a healthy family that aren't really all that necessary.

Now, let's mix up a new batch of family health, starting with food, glorious food!

Eating Strong — What you put inside your body has a direct impact on how you look and feel. Eating a healthy diet is a way to strengthen your immunity shield.

When it comes to food, my rule is to keep things simple and basic. By "simple", I actually mean "natural." My family used to eat a lot differently than we do now, and it had a definite impact on our overall health. It took us a while to figure out that our daughter Kayley had a lot of food allergies. When I say a lot of food allergies, I'm not exaggerating — it is easier to list off the things she *can* eat. Interestingly, when we started cooking for Kayley, we ate simpler, and Kayley was better off with her allergies. Our diet became one of unprocessed meats, fresh fruits and vegetables, rice and potatoes and some dairy. We omitted pretty much everything else. Back to basics.

I used to buy a lot of prepared sauces and packaged foods that were designed to help my food taste better. It just didn't seem right to eat chicken with a few spices, or steamed broccoli, naked on its own. I was forced into adapting a more natural food plan for my family, but in the end, I believe this kind of diet is the right choice for all families, even those without any allergy sufferers. We all need to eat outside the boxes and get back to our gardens and other natural foods.

So, what do we eat around here?

Well, I tend to cook a lot of "stir-fries" since you can use so many different varieties of vegetables and meats. If I want to add a sauce to the stir-fry, I'll dish out a sauce-free portion for my middle daughter first. Sometimes I prepare the food without sauce and then bring a variety of sauces to the table. This method allows everyone to add whatever sauce they like — personalizing meals is a way to encourage kids to feel more involved with their food, especially if they are not the ones doing the cooking. It's a good opportunity to teach them not to douse their plate in sauce so they can appreciate the taste of the food. If you do this right from the time your kids are young, they will really learn to love the taste of vegetables and other foods. When it comes to veggies, I steam everything! I love the crispness of steamed vegetables, and that they maintain their nutritional value.

Soups are another excellent way to get your veggies. The smaller you cut things up (you can even puree), the less horrifying the veggies are to your children. There's a cookbook out there right now called *Deceptively Delicious*, in which author Jessica Seinfeld (Jerry's better half) explains how to sneak nutritious foods into regular meal items.

I will routinely grind up spinach or kale in my mini food processor and add it to spaghetti sauce, homemade pizzas or taco meat and my kids eat it up! Once it's all mushed up and added to the sauce they don't even know that you are packing their food full of vitamins!

Talk to your children often about being healthy and what eating healthy food will do for them. Tell them that the protein in meat and eggs and beans helps to build strong muscles and that carrots are good for their eyesight. Help them learn early on how to take care of their own bodies properly and why it's important.

I remind my children all the time that it's not good to eat too much sugar, since it "knocks out" your immune system for 20 minutes. I explain it to my kids in a way that they can understand, like: "Sugar puts your body's soldiers to sleep, then the germs are able to sneak up more easily and attack!" Keep these discussions age-appropriate, but do not be afraid to use real, scientific words with your children either. They are sponges and will be able to "pick up what you're putting down." Treat them like people, instead of babies. Talk intelligently to them.

When you go grocery shopping, try to stay on the perimeter of the store and do your best not to venture up and down the middle aisles. The most natural, whole-food items are usually found around the edges of the grocery store — your meats, fresh produce, eggs and dairy. The middle aisles normally contain processed food items and cleaning products (ugh... I feel sick just walking down those intense-smelling aisles). I am in no way telling you what to eat — just to consider that when it comes to food, a back-to-basics mentality is important. We have been trained to eat packaged foods. We are rushed, busy and stressed and we neglect to plan to feed ourselves. Packaged foods are easy — "They're quicker, they'll save you time!" At least they're marketed to us that way.

Try, just for a while to omit packaged foods from your diet. I dare you. I *triple dare you*. It is really hard to do, but it is an enlightening experience. You may not be able to sustain this practice, but try it for at least one grocery shop (and then send me an e-mail telling me all about it, ShoppingDare@BeThatGirlNow.com).

Read the labels on the foods you buy whenever you can. The fewer ingredients on the package, the better, and being able to pronounce the ingredients is usually a bonus. Purchase locally sourced foods whenever possible and if you can, purchase "organic" produce to avoid ingesting pesticides. Eat fruits and vegetables that are in season in your area. Eating strawberries in winter requires some "special" gardening — maybe not as natural as it could be.

The Environmental Working Group (EWG) puts out a "Dirty Dozen" list of the Top 12 fruits and vegetables that should be bought organic based on the amounts of pesticides used by producers and other unhealthy growing practices (ewg.org/food-news/summary). This list changes yearly. This year (2013) the list grew to 14 and included the following:

- Apples
- Celery
- Cherry tomatoes
- Cucumbers
- Grapes
- Bell peppers
- Nectarines
- Peaches
- Potatoes
- Spinach
- Strawberries
- Kale/Collard Greens
- Summer Squash/Zucchini

The ideal situation, of course, is to grow your own fruits and vegetables, or shop on the weekends at Farmers' Markets where you can find locally grown meats, vegetables and baking (Yummm...*homemade cinnamon buns*).

"You-Pick" farms are also an excellent way to acquire locally grown produce, as well as being a fun weekend outing for the whole family. Drive out to the orchard or farm, typically located a short distance from where you are and then everyone picks fresh fruits and veggies together. You end up with pails of berries to make pies, jams, or just eat on the ride home, plus you are supporting your local farmers. Fun, delicious and nutritious!

I believe we have lost sight of how important eating really is and we have lost focus on what it truly means to feed ourselves. Working in the fields every day, tending to our gardens and livestock has been replaced with frozen microwave dinners and fast-food drive-thru lanes. Feeding yourself should be a priority in your day and you should plan your day around it. Make sure to give yourself enough time to nourish your body.

Most moms are the dinner planners in their households. (Yes, I know there are some out there with chef husbands or partners. We don't need to hear your bragging!) If it is your role to captain the food team (there must be a leader) then take great pride in this role. You are the one empowered with giving your family fuel to keep the fun fires burning. I know, it is a big responsibility, but it can be done easily if you keep it simple.

For years I have relied on author Sandi Richard's *Cooking for the Rushed* cookbooks (cookingfortherushed.com/new) to "meal plan" my life. If you dread the thought of making grocery lists and trying to figure out what to have for dinner, and find yourself getting frustrated because once you have decided what you want for dinner, you realize you don't have everything you need to make it, Sandi has got you covered. Her cookbooks detail weekly dinners that are nutritious and delicious and the directions are laid out in a way that anyone can follow along. There are also (*gasp!*) online printable grocery lists for each week of meals. Yes, meal planning can be just that simple. You will always know what you're having and you will have what you need to make it on hand.

Once you've started using Sandi's books, it's easy to start involving your family in the cooking process. Her method of meal planning helps you create a feeding schedule, whereby you can plan for your meals and groceries on a weekly basis, then, each night, you can plan out what meal you will be having the follow-

Any one of Sandi's Cookbooks are a great place to start for meal planning and getting you to the table as a family. Her latest book, "Anyone can Cook Dinner" is focused on getting your teens in on getting everyone to the table!

ing day. I can already feel the calmness in you that comes from knowing you are prepared for dinner the next day. Sandi calls it "eating forward" — when you know in advance what you're having for dinner, it's easier to plan what to eat during the day. If you've been stressing about food, it's time to check out Sandi's line of books. Just start with one and try it out for one week of meals. Then tell me about your experiences. I want to hear all about it!

As moms, it seems like we're always worried about what our kids are eating — or not eating. The last thing you want to do with your kids is instill in them a negative opinion about food. Setting food timers, force feeding, getting angry and worrying too much about the number of bites they put in their mouths can make dinnertime a rough part of the day for everyone. Food is essential for them to survive, but learning to love and appreciate healthy food will allow them to thrive.

Here are some tried-and-true tips to make "feeding time" more fun for your kids and more rewarding for you:

- **Institute the "One Bite Rule."** (This can also be applied to new activities) – The idea that they must try everything once before they are allowed to tell you they don't like it. Allow your children to have an open mind when it comes to food. Their taste buds are way more sensitive than ours and it may take them some time to acquire tastes. We adults, on the other hand, have long destroyed our taste buds or made them less sensitive over time! If you encourage kids to take one bite of something, even if they think it looks disgusting or that they will hate it, and then you tell them that they do not have to eat anymore after that one bite, they will be more open to try other things. In our house, a "bite" means chew and swallow. Just tell them to chase it with water if it is something they do not particularly enjoy.

- **Do NOT cook different things for each family member,** unless someone has an allergy. The easiest way to create a picky eater is to cater to them, giving them only what they like to eat and not encouraging them to eat other things. In our house, what is on the table is dinner. "You get what you get and you don't get upset," is our motto in regards to anything.

- **Making a game of anything makes it more fun.** If my kids eat everything on their plate but leave one thing (like their broccoli), I tell them their broccoli is sad that they are not eating it (this never fails to make them smile). Encourage them to take one bite of things and, when they do, cheer loudly and clap. Give them a high-five and tell them how happy the broccoli is now! Then tell them how excited the rest of the broccoli is just thinking about them eating more of it... The sillier you are, the more fun eating becomes. The goal is to make eating healthy things a positive experience. Try really hard not to be negative about their food habits, ever. Let your kids decide how much they want to eat. You provide them with healthy options and they decide how much they will eat. Trust me, your kids will not starve to death.

- **The smaller things are, the more kids seem to love them.** This includes sandwiches (cut them into silly shapes, or just cut them up into small pieces) and pancakes (our kids always fight over the small ones). Cookie cutters can shape pretty much any food into something cool-looking. Make smiley faces on their pancakes with fruit, or make smiley faces or hearts or initials with ketchup on their plates. Even healthy food can be fun and silly!

Eating Right from Morning to Night — It's important to eat breakfast as a family. Ideally, you want a well-rounded breakfast incorporating whole grains, fruits, veggies (if your kids will eat them), smoothies and protein (eggs, meats, yogurt). Really though, as long as you get something into your kids before they rush out to meet the bus in the morning, you will be doing great! (*You mean you don't have a full service breakfast buffet at your house every morning?*) (Try to feed everyone (including yourself) within an hour of waking up. All of you have essentially starved through the night, and if you do not feed your bodies first thing in the morning they begin to conserve fat. The body is smart enough to save itself; if it thinks it is starving, it will hang onto fat for dear life.

Lunches — the mere mention of this word sends any mother into a frenzy! Making lunches everyday is a chore that is not often rewarded, especially when your kids or partner are eating their lunch at work or school.

Here's my way of handling weekly lunches so that mornings are a breeze:

As soon as your kids come home from school, have them unpack their lunch containers. Be sure to have a water bottle for each kid that can be rinsed out and cleaned daily, and then refilled with water for the next day. Make a point of preparing lunches the night before. If you have time as soon as the kids get home from school, have them help you make lunches before you start supper. Kids of every age can help with filling water bottles, spreading jam on sandwiches, or getting fruits out and washing them.

Make lunches for EVERYONE in the family: your spouse or partner, your kids and yourself. If you stay at home for lunch, that's perfectly OK. At least now you'll know what you are having and it will make it even easier to enjoy a nice lunch break. If you don't have time before supper to get the next day's lunches made, then as soon as the supper dishes are done have everyone pitch in to get the lunches made and in the fridge before bedtime. This way, you know that everyone in your family has a healthy meal with them. Using this method greatly reduces the amount of money spent on take-out lunch foods and having healthy food on hand when they need it helps everyone maintain a good metabolism.

Here are some fantastic ideas for things to pack in your family's lunches:

- **The good ol' sandwich!** I use hard-case reusable containers for sandwiches, which makes it really easy to pack and makes sure they don't get squishy. Try to use a variety of breads and fillings so that you and your kids don't get too bored. Lunchmeats, tuna, egg salad, and jellies. Switching it up keeps lunchtime interesting. Add veggies like lettuce, tomato, sprouts, cucumbers etc. to sandwiches whenever you can. Try switching up the bread to a tortilla shell, or pita pocket for even more variety.
- **Cut-up fruits.** There is just something about having your fruit cut up for you. An apple cut up into segments is so much more desirable than a whole apple (plus, if you have a large family, the fruit goes farther when it is cut up). If anyone has wiggly teeth or braces or you are concerned about choking with younger kids, cut-up fruit is the only way to go.
- **Veggies, veggies, veggies.** Baby carrots, cut-up regular carrots, celery sticks, cherry tomatoes, snap peas, cucumbers, peppers, broccoli, cauliflower: cut-up veggies of all kinds. Include a small container of ranch dressing for dipping if your kids like that.
- **Yogurt.** Eat it with nuts or granola for an empowering afternoon snack (nuts are not allowed at most schools but YOU can eat them). Dried fruits are also great energy boosters.

- **Cut up cheese with rolled lunchmeats and crackers.**
- **Granola bars** (nut-free).
- **Soups** (send them for lunch in an insulated thermos).
- **Smoothies**
- **Salads** are terrific way to add veggies to your daily diet and keep you going. Roast and slice up a few chicken breasts to add extra protein. Nuts and dried fruits are also great in salads.
- **Hard-boiled eggs** are another excellent way to add protein to your lunch. It's nature's hand-food. Peeled in advance, it's such a neat-and-tidy little snack.

Having lots of fruits and vegetables in your lunches will keep you and your family energized. I also believe in eating small portions throughout the day — as your body needs it — rather than designating one time to sit and eat a large meal. For example: if you eat some fruit in the mid-morning, (around the same time that the kids are at recess), then eat a sandwich or salad at lunchtime, then yogurt, a granola bar or a handful of veggies around 2 p.m., you likely will not suffer the three-o'clock slump. You are giving your body little bits of energy to process and use throughout the day, and you are giving yourself little breaks throughout your day. We need to prioritize feeding ourselves with vitamin-rich food and wash it down with life-giving water!

Water Works —Water is an absolute essential for a healthy body and most of us already know we need to drink more of it. Drinking water helps flush toxins out our bodies and replenishes any water that we have expended throughout the day. Drinking enough fluids will also keep you feeling slightly full, making you less likely to snack throughout the day. Drinking enough fluids is a surefire way to kick start any "body beautifying" program, and it will also ensure that your immune system (your body's "soldiers") have enough stamina.

So why is it so difficult for us to drink enough water? I don't know the scientific answer to this, but in my opinion, I think it is because water doesn't have a taste and most of us are flavor junkies. So while drinking pure water is an excellent way to get your fluids, here are a few other things you can do to make water more fun:

- **Change up the temperature.** Drink room temperature or hot water instead of freezing-cold water. Warm drinks are thought to be better for your body as your bodily fluids are similarly warm. Just as hot drinks are relaxing, cold drinks are stimulating. Introducing freezing-cold water into your body can be a shock to your system and your body will burn calories to heat up this cold water to a temperature that it can process. While this calorie burning may seem like a good idea if you're trying to shed a few pounds, it can also be considered wasted energy. Hot drinks stimulate digestion, while cold water with a meal may actually slow down digestion. Warmer water arrives in your system ready for the body to use and it helps break food down faster. Cold water can solidify fats rather than breaking them down, making it harder for the body to purge those fats. If you want to make a simple change that will help you maintain a healthier lifestyle, drink more hot water (start with room temperature water if the idea seems weird). As an added bonus, boiled water is usually cleaner than cold water as some of the impurities are removed through the boiling process.
- **Drink herbal tea.** Herbal teas are delicious and they definitely count towards your daily water intake. Herbal teas can also be used as natural "healers." Peppermint tea after dinner will relieve bloated tummies, ginger tea can calm an upset stomach, chamomile tea will help you feel calmer and more relaxed before bed, and lemon tea can ease a sore throat. Kids love herbal tea. Try sending them to school with cooled tea in their water bottles once in a while for a nice change.
- **Always keep a "to-go" cup or bottle of water with you** wherever you go and be sure to send your kids to school with a full bottle of water or herbal tea. Juice boxes should be

considered a treat, in the same sense as cookies or a candy bar. Fruit juices have a ton of sugar. I am a strong advocate of drinking and driving as long as the drinking is water or tea! Driving forces us to sit still. Use this time to sip from your water bottle.

- **Make "spa water"** by adding fruits, veggies and herbs – just like they do at fancy hotels. Use oranges, lemons, strawberries, raspberries, blueberries, etc. Even just one of the above is delicious. Peeled cucumbers and herbs like mint are also refreshing. Put the fruits or veggies in a glass jar or pitcher, then it fill up with water. Let it stand on counter and fill your water bottles throughout the day. Each time you take some water out of your spa-water pitcher, fill it up with more water (if you have time!). If you prefer your drinks cold just add ice cubes. You can reuse the fruit and replenish with water for up to 48 hours and then the fruit should be tossed. Repeat with some new fruits!
- **Drink smoothies or veggie juices.** Yep, these count as "fluids." With all the amazing varieties and combinations, drinking your vitamins has never been so easy or delicious.
- **Limit your coffee, pop and juice intake.** If you're going to drink something, try to make it non-caffeinated and sugar-free whenever possible.

Food and water are essentials when it comes to keeping you and your family healthy, but they are not all you need to survive. If you want to maintain an energetic, healthy, happy family, you have got to add some of the other key ingredients.

BE THAT
MOM™

· · · · · · · · · · · · · · · · · · · ·

"The best years of your life are the ones
in which you decide your problems are your
own. You do not blame them on your mother,
the ecology, or the president. You realize
that you control your own destiny."

— *Albert Ellis*

· · · · · · · · · · · · · · · · · · · ·

CHAPTER 7

The Naturally Healthy Family

· · · · · · · · · · · · · · · · · ·

"Early to bed and early to rise,
makes a man healthy, wealthy and wise!"
– Benjamin Franklin

A healthy family is one that gets the right amount of rest. Our bodies need an incredible amount of rest to regenerate, heal and protect us. When your family is well rested, you will all be able to fight off nasty germs and deal with stress more productively. It's time to start waking up on the right side of the bed every day!

Tuning Out and Tucking In — Speaking of sleep, how tired are you right now on a scale of one to 10? Are you fighting back yawns while reading this book? Well, I'd like to think it's not me and instead, it's just because you need to get more sleep. Yes, I'm sure that's what it is...

Sleep is so, so important, for you and your children. It's essential for good health and peace of mind. The earlier you teach your children healthy sleep routines, the better off they will be. The same goes for you — not getting enough sleep can make you sick, which makes everything in life harder. If you are not sleeping well, you need to find ways to sleep better.

No matter what age your children are, it's important that they are getting enough sleep and that this sleep is uninterrupted over the course of the night. Right now, our children are nine, seven and five years old, and it's extremely rare for any of them to awake during the night. My husband and I are the same way. It happens maybe once or twice in a year…and it has been that way for years. It is an *expectation* that everyone sleeps through the night in our house, not just a fleeting hope.

Our secret is that we actively sleep-trained our children right from birth. That's right, we trained them to sleep well. The method we used was taken from a book that I consider my "sleep bible:" *Healthy Sleep Habits, Healthy Child* by Mark Weissbluth.

Here are some of key points that have worked great for me and my family:

> **Tune out.** Make sure you tune out of all electronics one hour before bed. TV can be incredibly stimulating, especially for kids, and it can negatively affect their ability to get a good night's sleep. The imagery on TV is not just unicorns and rainbows these days – you're likely to see all manner of violent police procedurals, car chases, monsters and zombies, even on prime-time channels. What you watch right before you go to bed creates some rather interesting brainwaves. Those images may be affecting you and your family's ability to get the rejuvenating sleep you all need, so tune out a bit before bed.

> **Establish a bedtime routine.** For your kids, the routine might go something like this: bath time, jammy time, teeth time, story time, potty time, bed time. For you, it may be wash your face, brush your teeth, and read a good book in bed, or in a cozy, quiet spot as a way to relax before you go to sleep. It's important to prepare your body for sleep. When you have a routine in place, everyone understands what comes next, and you will find it easy to get your kids nicely tucked into bed, do your own thing for a while, and then get yourself a good night's sleep as well.

Establish sleep rules for your household (the following have been adapted from Weissbluth's book).

1. When it is bedtime, you go to bed and you don't get out of your bed.
2. You keep your eyes closed.
3. You be quiet.
4. You go to sleep, and you sleep until morning.

If your kids get out of their beds, deny them any attention for doing so. Don't look at them or talk to them, just keep putting them back in their beds, as it is now bedtime. Your children will learn soon enough that when it's bedtime, playtime is over. In fact, once your children have been sleep trained, you might find them asking you to put them to bed when they are ready! That is the beauty of having your children appreciate and understand when they need to sleep. I highly recommend reading Weissbluth's book for more details on how to help your children develop better sleeping patterns *at any age.*

Feng Shui can also play a key role in peaceful and satisfying sleep habits. If your children (or you) are having trouble sleeping, take a look at the bedroom's Feng Shui, or energy flow. Keep in mind that bedrooms are meant to be relaxing sanctuaries where our bodies can rejuvenate and recharge in preparation for more exciting adventures. Bedrooms should be painted soft, calming colors, display calming artwork and be clutter free. If your kids have a lot of toys or books in their rooms, they will find this very stimulating and distracting, and, rather than wanting to sleep, they may want to play. Minimize the amount of "stuff" in your child's room. Ensure there is no clutter underneath the bed. Keep the bedside tables neat and tidy with only book on them at a time. Keep toys in closets, keep closet doors closed and remove any mirrors. Electronics in the bedroom are not good Feng Shui, however, if you are committed to having them in bedrooms, be sure they can be closed away at night. Keep your child's room door closed and be sure it is dark enough to encourage sleeping — blackout blinds are a fantastic invention!

Natural Healing

Moms definitely need to be flexible. You just never know when the chicken pox, fever, a broken arm, the 24-hour flu or a boo-boo are going to pop up and change the plans you originally had for your day (or your entire week). Moms are usually the ones who have to drop everything when their kids need them. This is why being a working mom can be so difficult (and why employers need to be more flexible also).

As "That Mom," you must prepare for the unexpected. Things are going to change all the time, and other things are going to come up without warning. You must fortify yourself mentally to handle what comes your way. Don't cry over spilled milk, rather think to yourself, "It's just milk… it can be cleaned up… it's not the end of the world."

When the inevitable happens and someone in your home gets sick or hurt, I would encourage you to turn to natural solutions for healing. I'm a big proponent of the natural medicine cabinet and homeopathic remedies. You need to be aware of everything you are putting in your body and in the bodies of your family — especially when it comes to medicine. It's crucial that you do your research. Rather than zooming off to the doctor or hospital every time you experience a basic ailment, there's a good chance that there is an alternative treatment that can be done easily and in the comfort of your own home.

Whenever my children or I have an issue, I go online (unless I already know what to do). A basic search of "homeopathic remedies for (insert your condition or symptoms)" will bring up a variety of suggestions. You will likely have to weed through some crappy information before you find a treatment that you can actually use. Be aware that the Internet should not replace the professional opinion of a medical doctor, or naturopath. Also, be aware that you can easily freak yourself out and end up thinking you have a much more serious problem (the Internet can really foster hypochondria, even in sensible people).

I recently suffered a urinary tract infection and wanted to see what I could do naturally to cure it. Cranberry juice and cranberry pills were the most common suggestions but I didn't have immediate access to those things, so I kept looking. Then, I stumbled upon something that seemed intriguing on the site **www.myhomeremedies.com**. The instructions were to: "Peel a granny smith apple; pour some white vinegar into a dish and add salt; dunk the apples in the vinegar, mix and then eat them; then drink the vinegar." The remedy promised that symptoms should start to subside within an hour.

This treatment made sense to me, since I was already aware of the healing properties of apple-cider vinegar and how changing the pH of the body can have a dramatic effect on your health. I had everything I needed, so I tried it. Surprisingly, it tasted great (your body sometimes just knows what you need). More importantly, it actually worked! No antibiotics for this girl!

Obviously, you must seek help from a medical doctor if you cannot cure something yourself. You might also want to visit a naturopathic doctor, or homeopathic practitioner before visiting a medical doctor. The body is an amazing organism and you will find yourself surprised and in awe of how it can be healed naturally.

I started dabbling in natural medicines when my first daughter, Trinity, had a recurring ear infection. We had gone through two rounds of antibiotics and it still came back! One of my friends recommended we try treating it with silver. At that point, I was game to try anything. I found my way to a natural health store where the staff encouraged me to get the "silver kit," which included a dropper that we could use to dose the silver into Trinity's ear. Needless to say, the silver cured the ear infection and she's never had one like it since. Now, anytime the girls or anyone else in our family has a sore ear, we treat it with a few drops of silver right away and I normally don't "hear" a thing about it again (no pun intended).

After that ear infection was cured, the silver and the applicator bottle sat in my medicine cabinet. I had no idea at the time how to use silver to its full potential until that same friend told me how it could be used instead of antibiotic creams and ointments, like Polysporin. I decided it was time for me to find out more, so I took to my favorite resource — the Internet. The list of things silver can be used to treat was shocking and amazing and I immediately set about researching other natural remedies. I've also expanded my knowledge about natural remedies by simply asking questions at my local health food store. The staff are so knowledgeable about the products and eager to share the secrets of natural healing with anyone who will listen.

As moms, we want to do what's best for our kids and will do anything to relieve their pain, or help them get better from an illness. I've certainly experienced that with our second daughter. Kayley has always struggled with multiple allergies and her skin reflected these allergies with a bad case of eczema. Kayley was always itchy, and her poor little face was always red. For a while, we used regular allergy medicine to control her reactions — basically, an antihistamine for children. The medicine always worked for her allergies, but it made her drowsy and I hated the thought of constantly medicating her. I inquired about alternate medicines at the health food store and was introduced to an amazing natural allergy pill that is safe for anyone to use, called Pascallerg. These "chewable-if-required" pills work like a charm, have no side effects, and best of all, I never have to worry about accidentally overdosing my child! I like to be conscious about what I am putting into my body and my children's bodies.

The Natural Medicine Cabinet — If you're thinking about dabbling in Natural Medicine, here are a few essential items that I like to have on hand at all times. If you're new to natural medicines, just read this list over and pick one that you think you might need the most. Make it a point to visit a natural foods and health store and simply ask for the product. Try using it once or twice in place of what you normally use to treat a certain condition to see how you feel and what results you get. As with anything, when you shift to something new, it can feel uncomfortable at first, so ease into it. I am confident that once you experience great success, you will be coming back for more. The list will be here for you to use, as you are ready.

"Colloidal" or "Ionic" Silver — This is usually sold as a liquid in a few different sizes (though I would recommend buying a larger bottle as it has a lot of uses). As for the difference between "colloidal" and "ionic," I have asked a variety of health-store staffers and received conflicting information about which type is better. What I would recommend is to start with whichever one your store carries — or the cheaper of the two if they carry both. Either one will work, so don't worry...(be happy!) You will also want to acquire a "silver accessory kit," consisting of three glass bottles, one with a press-spray lid, one with a dropper and one that looks like a nasal sprayer. No, it is not cheap, but you will get your money's worth, and you'll only ever have to buy it once. Buy dark glass containers whenever possible and not clear bottles, as light can affect your remedies.

Pour some of your silver into each bottle so that you can use it appropriately (you may need to drop some into an eye or ear, spray some of it onto a cut or into the back of your throat, or spray it into your nasal passage). *Never use a metal spoon, or any other metal when you are dosing with silver, as the metal will counteract the silver and it won't work.* I use a small medicine cup or a plastic measuring spoon. Silver is a natural antibiotic so it can be used for almost anything. Before you run to traditional medicines, always consider the option of using silver first. Be sure to read the bottle for dosage instructions.

Here are a few common uses for silver:

- Eye, ear, nose and throat infections: orally and dose directly into the orifice. Use one-to-two drops for eyes and ears (applied directly) and also take orally, per bottle directions.
- Colds and flu: take orally. In the case of a sore throat, spray the back of the throat a few times as well as take orally.
- Cuts, sunburns and rashes: use to stimulate healing. Also effective on insect bites — spray silver directly on the affected area.
- Acne: apply topically.
- Wart removal and nail-fungus treatment: spray onto affected area twice daily. If you worry about bacteria at the nail salon, just give a quick spray of silver to your nails when you get home as a preventative measure.
- Kitchen disinfectant: works as a germ-killer on cutting boards and counter surfaces. Can also be used on phones and keyboards as an antibacterial agent.
- Purification: add a few drops to water if you are unsure of its purity.

Arnica Gel and Arnica Pellets —Arnica promotes healing of damaged tissue and is best used for muscle pain, bumps and bruises. Take the pellets orally and/or apply the gel right to the affected area. I took it immediately following childbirth and was amazed at how fast and effective it was at relieving my pain. I also use it on my children's bumps and bruises. It is not to be used on open wounds, so if you have a cut, use something else, like silver or calendula.

Homeopathic Pellets — When it comes to most homeopathic pellets, the standard dose for most remedies is three. Remedies are most effective when you do not eat or drink anything but water for 20 minutes before and 20 minutes after taking them. Morning and night tend to be the best times to take the pellets and evening dosages tend to be the most effective, likely because the body is resting. The pellet containers are designed so that you can easily turn the top of the lid and get the right dose into the cap. Remove the cap, and dump into your mouth. *Do NOT touch the homeopathic pellets with your fingers;* just pour them right into your mouth using the cap. Tuck the pellets under your tongue and allow them to dissolve on their own. I know these yummy little sugary pellets taste good, but it's best to try not to chew them up. With homeopathic remedies, normally one dose is enough to do the trick. If it doesn't work, you may actually need a different remedy. Either way, read the package and consult your natural health store for more information.

Calendula Gel and Tincture — Use this remedy on cuts, scrapes and skin irritations like sunburn. Calendula can replace common antibiotic ointments. It's extremely effective in healing skin. Calendula can also be found in creams, as a gel and as a tincture. The gel is very cooling and it will not sting like some other items you may have put on your children's cuts. The gel is an essential item for

your natural medicine cabinet and an excellent place to start. The tincture is a liquid form of calendula that can be mixed with water and used as a rinse to promote healing to the skin. There are some hand creams on the market that have calendula in them that are great for healing extremely dry, cracked skin.

Pascallerg Allergy Pills — Improper dosage of mainstream allergy and cold medications can have serious side effects for children, so I am reluctant to give them to my family. Pascallerg (made by a company called Pascoe) is a natural allergy pill that doesn't cause drowsiness or have any other adverse side affects. It works like a charm for kids and adults with food, animal or environmental allergies. The pills have little-to-no taste and are easily chewed up

by children or adults who can't take swallowing a pill whole. If you, or someone in your family suffers from allergies, I would encourage you to try out Pascallerg as an alternative and see if it works for you.

Oil of Oregano — I'm not going to mince words here... this stuff tastes awful, but it sure is effective in killing germs! Use it for skin conditions, digestive problems, and sinus congestion or to ward off an oncoming cold or flu. You can take it straight up by just dropping it in your mouth (cringe), or you can mix it with some water, or other beverage and "shoot it." My kids detest this stuff but if any

of us are fighting a cold, and silver just isn't doing it, we'll resort to oil of oregano. You can tell by the taste of this stuff that it's powerful! Read the bottle for dosage information and do not take if you are pregnant.

Camilia (New Mom Tip!) — This stuff is an amazing natural teething remedy. Camilia is a liquid that comes in small plastic tubes. Just twist off the tip and drop right into baby's mouth. It tastes just like water and best of all, relieves those aching gums. Babies love it! Read package for dosage instructions.

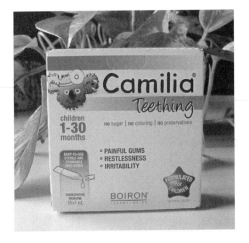

Apis Gel (also called Dapis Gel by some companies) — Use this stuff on mosquito, spider and other insect bites, as well as wasp, hornet and bee stings. It's a great thing to have at home, but a MUST

for camping and travelling. If anyone in the family is bitten or stung, immediately apply apis gel to the bite. The apis gel will relieve the swelling while helping to remove any foreign bacteria that may have been left by the insect. If there is a stinger left in the skin, remove it using tweezers before applying the apis gel. Never leave home without it!

Nux Vomica — This remedy for upset stomach, food poisoning and bloating comes in pellet form. It's definitely one of those things to keep on hand at home, and to make sure you have packed in your travel bag. At the first sign of any stomach-related issues, dose with this remedy. Nothing is worse than being on vacation as a

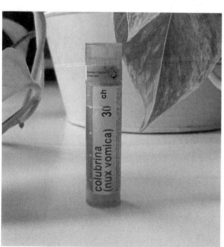

family and having someone get sick to their stomach and having to be in bed or on the toilet for days. This remedy works really well for food-related or travel-related sickness. Ask your natural health store for dosage recommendations.

Tea Tree Oil — This is an anti-fungal remedy that can be used for a variety of issues like athlete's foot, yeast infections, acne, or toenail fungus. It is for external use only and should never be taken orally. Tea tree oil is also a great antiseptic and I often use a couple drops in a bowl of boiling water to clean hairbrushes or nail tools.

Tea Tree Oil can be used as an ingredient in making your own baby wipes. (See Chapter 1, Baby Mine for details). With just a handful of facecloths, an airtight container and a few natural ingredients, you can omit "baby wipes" from your shopping list and say goodbye to all those chemicals on your baby's bum. As an added bonus, you can feel good about sparing the environment your baby wipe trash. Imagine if everyone used cloth diapers and reusable homemade wipes instead of disposable diapers for their babies? The sheer amount of waste that we produce as a society could be exponentially reduced from this one small shift (Oh, how I love to dream about ways that the world could reduce its output of garbage. I am a nut about this!).

Natural Travel Vaccines —You can literally travel the world without ever having to get a needle for a travel vaccination. We often travel to Roatan, Honduras on account of a close family connection there. The first time we went, I was concerned for my family's safety regarding all the diseases to which they might be exposed. I popped in to see my homeopath and she brewed us up vaccinations appropriate for Honduras, covering malaria, hepatitis, yellow fever, and typhoid, along with detailed instructions on how to take them. I packed them with us on our trip and we were

No need to get a bunch of shots when you are ready to travel the world. Your natural health provider can help you with some natural vaccinations that can protect you over the duration of your trip. Do your own research to find out what is required for the places you will be travelling to, and then have your naturopath prepare the vaccines for you and your family.

protected the entire time, without anyone getting a shot — happy mom, happy kids, healthy family!

So that wraps up my list of the primary items that should be in every natural-medicine cabinet. Additional items can be obtained on an as-need basis. It's awesome to have a little collection of remedies with you. The easiest way to remember what a remedy ought to be used for (i.e.: eye infection, bladder infection, food poisoning, sun stroke, snake bite, etc.) is to write on the remedy with a pen. Of course, you can always turn to the Internet to find out what remedy is best used for various symptoms. Often, there are a number of remedies that will work for a particular set of symptoms and you may have just what you need with you already. Also, develop a relationship with your natural health food store and its employees, so you can steal their insight! Fake it 'til you make it — naturally!

More great tips for family health... When you're out having fun in the summertime, protect your family from the harmful rays of the sun using **chemical-free, all-natural sunscreen** as well as proper clothing and sun hats. Your whole family should also be taking Vitamin D drops. A good friend advised me to keep Vitamin D drops in the bathroom with the toothbrushes, so that administering them to everyone in the family becomes part of the daily routine. That tip has helped my family become more regular with our D vitals! *Speaking of being regular…*

Shit, Or Get Off The Pot — Regular and healthy bowel movements (BMs) are a sure sign your body is functioning as it should. Food goes in, waste goes out. It is a beautiful cycle that works great when the right things are put into it. The faster your body can process what you put in and dispel of any stuff that's not required, the better it is for you. "Better out than in, I always say…" (words of wisdom from none other than Shrek!). The water, fruits and fibre we consume work to keep things moving. Some stomach-related issues are due to gas and the build up of waste products in the intestine, so when you keep things flowing, you keep yourself feeling great!

The optimum frequency for BMs varies widely. Some people have a BM after every meal, some once a day and some people every couple of days. Everyone is different in this area, but my advice would be to strive for once a day. Talk with your children about their regularity and tell them to let you know if there is anything funny in that department. I seem to recall an episode of Oprah that advised that a good BM was one that was solid and floated in the toilet — another thing to strive for in the bathroom?

You will know you are eating properly when you have regular BMs. Eat too much cheese, red wine and baguettes, and you will notice a major difference in your regularity. When your kids eat neon-coloured fruit roll-ups, they will likely notice that their BM's come out weirdly bright! When they ask you why, it's probably a good time to discuss food colourings.

Your BM should also be easy to manage. You should literally be able to sit, shit, and get off the pot! You should not have to sit on the toilet for 20 minutes. It's one thing if you *choose* to use your bathroom time to catch up on your book or magazine reading, but you should not have to expend much effort in that department. In fact, too much squeezing and sitting on the 'john' can cause hemorrhoids and other health issues. Taking probiotic supplements can be helpful in this area. Probiotics are essentially "good bacteria" that can help with digestion. Probiotic pills (which can be found at any natural or health food store), combined with a proper diet, will have you feeling good and regular in no time.

Judge your health by your BMs and if you are not satisfied with what you see and smell (or how you feel), take action now!

Don't Hold Back — As moms, some of us probably wish we could "hold back" our pee when jumping on trampolines, or laughing too hard. But that alone is the reason for regular bathroom breaks for yourself and your kids throughout the day. Never hold your urine or your BM longer than is necessary. I know we all get busy, but we need to expel our waste when our bodies tell us to, not when we feel like we have time. Kids are particularly bad for not wanting to take bathroom breaks — who wants to miss out on any of the fun to go to the bathroom? But holding in your urine for extended periods can stretch out your bladder, which can lead to incontinence. Holding in BM's can cause constipation. If you have issues using public toilets, you need to change your thinking. The health issues that can result from holding it in are not worth it. You must do what you can to go when the urge to go first arises, even if it means squatting over a public toilet or peeing in the grass.

Be that Healthy Mom with the healthiest kids around. You really can do it, and it's really not that hard. Just keep it simple, keep it natural, keep it regular, keep it scheduled and don't forget to have a little fun! Being healthy is a family affair and when you make it a priority to be good to your body, and good to the environment, you will all be feeling vibrant, energetic, slim and motivated. Life is good when you're healthy enough to enjoy it to the fullest. Start getting healthier by making a few small changes in your life and measure the results for yourself. Keep doing what works for you. You are an incredible Mom, taking such great care of your family.

Now — where have you been keeping your children warm, dry and safe, Momma Bear? Providing shelter for your family is another way we contribute to the health of our families. In some countries, just having a roof and walls to protect from the elements is admirable and to have heat and running water on top of that is a bonus. In North America, most of us are fortunate enough to be living in pretty decent 'shelters'. No matter where you are living, I am now going to take you on a journey full of energy and promise, health and wealth and efficiency. That journey will be through your home. Come with me and I will teach you some simple Feng Shui principles that can have a huge effect on every area of your life.

Let's get moving!

"Organizing is what you do
before you do something,
so that when you do it,
it is not all mixed up."

— *A. A. Milne*

CHAPTER 8

The Shelter

· · · · · · · · · · · · ·

"Absorb what is useful. Discard what is not.
Add what is uniquely your own."
– Bruce Lee

It's not where you live that makes a home a home... it's what you put into a home that makes a home. Whether it's family, love, furniture, food, clothes, shoes, or pets — home is really a place to keep you dry, warm, protected, and it doubles as a place to store your things. Busy families with jobs, chores and busy kids need to have a home space that is comforting, nourishing, and, most importantly, revitalizing. That is home.

Years ago, I was introduced to Feng Shui at a day long Women's Convention with my good friend, Sarah. In a one hour session, I was so intrigued and wanted to learn more. I bought a Feng Shui book and devoured it. I knew that I had found a new passion. Based upon the principles of energy flow, Feng Shui translates into 'Wind Water'. Every home, every room, every window, every piece of furniture, each piece of artwork, has its own energy, better known as Chi. The focus with Feng Shui is to welcome and encourage positive energy flow into your life, and to reduce, wherever possible, any negative energy flowing into your life. The things we choose to have around us are reflections of our inner selves and our inner selves are directly influenced by what we surround ourselves with.

Keeping that in mind, using the principles of Feng Shui in your external surroundings can enhance, improve and allow more of everything to flow into your life. The coolest part about Feng Shui is you can easily start applying it in your life right away! Feng Shui can be used in every part of your life: home, office, travelling, etc. Once you get a little taste of it, you will find yourself easily adapting things to suit a more efficient energy flow. For now, let's start in your home with some simple baby steps that you can take to get that positive chi rolling into your life.

Let's talk now about things, bling, toys, cars, boats, Panini grillers, bikes, shoes, your children's crafts, pictures, Christmas stuff, Easter stuff, Halloween stuff, birthday stuff, stuff, stuff, stuff! AAAAAHHHHHHHH!!!! It is amazing how much stuff we can accumulate in a very short period of time!

How's your clutter? Do you know exactly what is in every cupboard in your house? Do you use everything you own? When was the last time you cleaned out your clothes closet... or your purse?

Clutter is the enemy for a number of reasons. When there is clutter in your life, your subconscious mind will always be drawn to that negative pile of stuff. There will be no room in your mind, or in your life, for new, vibrant things to come in. Reducing the amount of things in your life will allow you to focus eagerly on the tasks at hand, while encouraging vitality in your home. Clearing out your clutter is a fantastic way to get energy flowing in your home and it is something that I get really excited about. I want you to get excited about clearing out your clutter, because it is going to set you free and change your life. You just have to trust me.

One way to avoid having clutter pile up in your life is to stick to the following rule:

Everything in your home must have a place. If the things you own have a designated space in your home, the items can be found quickly and easily and can be put back where they belong just as quickly, by anyone (even the littlest members of the family).

If you do not have a space for something in your home, do one of two things:

1. Get rid of the item. Throw it out or donate it as quickly as possible.
2. Get rid of something else in order to make room for the item you want to keep.

Be ruthless in determining which things you really need. If you do not have space for something, you must find one or out it goes! Moving to a larger home to accommodate all of your things should not be the goal. Working within the space you already have is your focus.

Now, let's tackle the clutter you do have in your home.

Clutter is just plain bad. It gives off the worst kind of negative energy! Eliminating negative energy is of extreme importance in your home and the easiest way to do that is to eliminate your clutter. WHERE your clutter is in your home can be having a very direct impact on very specific areas of your life. Clutter defined, is any accumulation of things in one area; it can be piles of things that need to be done, things that need repairing, things you don't need or use anymore, and anything that you have too much of/or not enough room for.

As with anything, learning something new can be exciting, uncomfortable, and often takes effort. If you want to create a home that is relaxing, tidy, organized, easy to maintain and functional, it will take a little work from you (and your family too). I will not force you to go through your entire home all at once. That would be cruel and I'm not that kind of girl. What I want you to do is get excited! Think about one area in your home that has been driving you crazy… that one place that you walk past and think "UUUrrggg, I really need to do something about that!" That's where we're going to start. I want you to focus on that space only and do not think about any other areas. The hardest part about clutter clearing is actually getting started with it. I mean, *who has 5 hours to clear clutter?* We overwhelm ourselves with the daunting task of doing our whole house and then we never get started on anything!

So, let's get back to that one place where you're going to start. This is going to be fun! Find a half an hour in your day and here's what you're going to do:

> **TIP:** These clutter clearing rules apply no matter what space you are working on, be it a whole room, a cupboard, a drawer, or a closet.
>
> **1.** Set a kitchen or egg timer based on the amount of time you have allocated to your project. If 30 minutes works for you, do that. If you have more time, or less, set it for your ideal. If you don't finish, you'll have to come back to it or create some extra time. No problem! Stop when the timer goes off.
>
> **2.** Gather up a handful of green garbage bags, a laundry basket or two, and /or a few empty boxes. Go to the space you intend to clear.
>
> **3.** Take everything out of the space you are clearing. I mean, everything!
>
> **4.** Assess each item. Use your bins (laundry basket , bags, or boxes) to sort each item into one of the following categories:

Keep It! Things that fall into this category will be one pile. If the item goes in the room you are working on, find a space for it right away — not shoved in a cluttered closet, but somewhere that it is easy to find, access and put away. Otherwise, leave it in the pile with the intention of finding a spot elsewhere. Once you are done clearing the space you are working on, you will put the items from this pile away in their new places. This will also help you determine which area will be your next project.

Trash It! This has become one of my favorite things to do. I am ruthless! If something is broken and not useable or able to be repaired, it needs to go in the garbage. Be honest... are you really going to mend those pants, or glue that Christmas ornament back together? Toss it and feel good about it. Unfinished projects get in the way of good energy. Trash it and move on!

Donate It! This is the give-away pile. I love donating stuff I don't need if someone out there can use it. This pile is for things that are still usable, but no longer have a place in your life. We have a clothes donation box close to our home that I frequent. It is so easy to do and doesn't take that long. I also love donating to Goodwill. Donating allows you to help others and when you come home to your organized space, you feel amazing too. It's a win-win situation!

Return It! If part of your clutter involves someone else's stuff that you have borrowed, or stuff that has ended up in your home some-how — put it all in a pile and then make time to return it to the rightful owners as soon as possible.

Sell It! Taking your useable items to a second-hand or consign-ment store opens up the possibility of earning money for your unwanted treasures. You can also use an online classified ad ser-vice like Kijiji to market used items. Include a picture of your item when you put it online — after all, a picture is worth a thousand words. You can also have a garage sale if you clean out every room in your house. Remember to price your items fairly if you'd like them to sell. (*I hate going to garage sales where people price their stuff really high and then won't budge on the price. Come on, people! You don't want the stuff* anymore, right?) I understand it can be hard to let go of items you may be emotionally attached to, so please use discretion of what's important.

Once you have all your stuff sorted and have put away the items that belong in that particular room, take the other piles out of that area. The stuff that you want to keep will now need to be given space in a different room. Put this pile somewhere like the kitchen, or another high-traffic area... where you will have no choice but to deal with it. Clear away the trash piles and the recycling to the garage, or the bin in the alley.

If you are dealing with the trash and donated items yourself, load them into your vehicle right away to make it easier for you to deal with on your next trip out. This action removes the clutter instantly from your home. If there are things that need to be returned to others, place the pile near the door to take with you or in the garage where you will see it on your next trip out. Or, make a point of setting up a time when the owner can drop by. Either way, the goal is to sort the clutter and then deal with it right away. You'll be inspired by feeling the satisfaction that comes from seeing these unwanted items reach the trash, recycling depot, second-hand store, donation box or rightful owners. Enjoy that feeling!

> "The best part about getting rid of 'things' is the process immediately allows for an abundance of new energy to flow into your life. Out with the old and in with the new! "
> – Tina O'Connor

The biggest thing to remember about clutter clearing is to *Never Stop* doing it! This is the most important thing you can do to achieve results in your life. Clearing clutter is an ongoing process and will require consistent action. At first it may seem like an impossible and never-ending task; eventually, you will make it through every room, nook, and cranny in your home. Once that happens, reorganizing and de-cluttering areas of your home will become a one-hour project here and there, whenever it happens to fit your schedule.

Here is the picture of a closet of mine that I featured in my first book, Be That Girl. This beautiful reorganization picture was taken in December 2011.

Taken in December of 2012, a whole year after my initial reorganization in Be That Girl, here is proof positive that even 'That Girl' has cupboards that get out of hand. One year later, and this cupboard needed me again! Organizing your home takes consistent effort.

As is my rule for any space, you have got to take everything out in order to assess the space you are working with.

What a delightful, organized space. You can see everything, and it is easy to access each item. I wonder if I can get another year out of this cupboard before I have to reorganize again!

Another good mantra to follow is... 'DO IT NOW!' If you see an area that bothers you, or a pile of stuff on the floor, don't just walk away from it and think: "I'll get to that later." That is how you ended up with clutter in the first place. Being That Mom requires you to be proactive and take action whenever you can. Teach your children the value of picking their stuff up off the floor and putting it where it belongs immediately. Remember, everything has a place, so everyone should know where it goes. It may take a little reminding (or a lot!), but soon enough, the joyous feeling of being clutter free will envelop your home like a cozy blanket and your children will miraculously start putting things where they belong. (*I made that sound pretty easy, eh?*) It may not be perfect, but it's going to get better for sure! Everyone in your home will be more relaxed, calm, and more full of the positive chi that will be flowing into your lives. Be prepared to enjoy your sanctuary a lot more. Your home will continue to be better and more efficient and you will start to see results in every other aspect of your life. It's up to you to get the ball rolling! **Set a timer and create something new right now!**

Be That Girl Secret: There is a difference between "Organized" and "Clean". The great thing about getting your home organized and tidy is that no one will notice if your home is not white glove clean. The perception will always be that your home is clean, even if it has been a couple of weeks since you scrubbed the place. "Cleaning" an organized space is also much easier than cleaning a cluttered space...another bonus!

The clutter clearing will be your ongoing project and as you clear each space, you should also take time to decide if everything in the room is where you would like it. More importantly, do the items in the room allow for fantastic Chi energy to flow smoothly, easily and gently into each room? Let's delve a little deeper into applying the principles of Feng Shui into each room of your home.

Let's start with a few basic Feng Shui rules:

1. **Round edges** are always a better than sharp corners. Energy can flow more easily around roundish corners; Sharp edges give off negative energy. From a safety perspective, it's pretty difficult to run into a round table and get hurt! Anything that your subconscious mind thinks can hurt you or someone you love, is not good Feng Shui. If you have sharp-edged furniture already, you can use a table cloth or other padded material, to cover the edges for a better flow and safer environment.

2. **Walking around in each room should be an easy thing to do.** You should not have to squeeze past things to avoid hurting yourself, and you should be able to easily access furniture used for sitting. Each room should encourage you to come into it and use it.

3. **The Power Position**– No matter what room you are in, or where you are, always strive to be in the 'power position'. You will know that you are in the 'power position' if you can see the door from where you are sitting or standing *and* you are not in direct alignment with the door, nor is your back to the door or a window. To describe this best, you want to be where you can see all the action and avoid being snuck up on by anyone or anything! Think about this when choosing a seat at the dinner table, sitting at your office desk, in an interview setting, with your bed placement. Think of it in every room of your house! Do not be afraid to be up front about what seat you want...it can have an amazing impact on your persuasiveness and confidence!

4. **Plants!** Plants have a way of adding life, energy, balance and health to any home. Plants are not only pleasing to the eye... they clean the air that we breathe! Plants suck up the negative energy and give off positive energy, just as they take in harmful gases and provide us with oxygen. Corners give off negative energy (in Feng Shui, this is referred to as "poisoned arrows"), so placing plants in the corners of rooms can significantly improve the energy in a room. Plants also suck up negative electrical energy, so be sure to use them around your electronic

equipment (close to your computer) and to cover up exposed electrical outlets and cables. Principles of Feng Shui say to avoid having prickly cactus plants in the home, as they are sharp, dangerous and do not promote good energy. Instead, choose plants with smooth, round leaves. Jade plants and Chinese Money plants make great choices for the wealth corner of your home. Bamboo, Schefelera, Dieffenbachia, Ficus and Peace Lily's are also believed to be good plants to have in your home. The Peace Lily (spathiphyllum) has smooth, rounded leaves, it grows beautiful white flowers and it is a very hardy plant easy for beginner plant lovers. The Peace Lily also has superior air cleaning capabilities, making this my first choice when it comes to house plants. Avoid having dried flowers in your home. Dried flowers are *dead* flowers, and you don't need that kind of energy in your life! Fake plants can also add good energy to your home, as long as they are kept clean and look real and vibrant. You will miss out on the air cleaning with fake plants, but it's better than nothing Use plants strategically in every room of your home and you will notice a difference in your mood.

The Bagua

Now that your home is clutter free and amazing, I want to pass on another exciting, easy-to-use Feng Shui tool called "The Bagua". The Bagua can be used as a decorating and item-placement guide throughout your entire home. When decorating, use your Bagua Map and you will see some amazing things happen in your life. The Bagua is a 9 section grid that is used to 'map' out different areas of your home.

According to the Bagua grid, each home can be divided into the following 9 areas:

Wealth and Prosperity   Creativity & Children

Fame & Reputation   Knowledge & Wisdom

Love & Relationships   Career

Family   Helpful People & Travel

Health & Well Being

I have included a copy of the Bagua below.

Wealth and Prosperity	Fame and Reputation	Love and Relationships
Wood	Fire	Earth
Blue, Purple and Red	Red	Pink, White and Red
Family	Health and Well-Being	Creativity and Children
Wood		Metal
Blue and Green	Earth	White
	Yellow	
Knowledge and Wisdom	Career	Helpful People and Travel
Earth	Water	Metal
Black, Blue and Green	Black	White, Grey and Black

becauseilive.hubpages.com/hub/FengShuiBagua

When you are aware which areas of your home correspond to the grids located on the Bagua, it can help you assess your family's current situation. Further, you will be able to stimulate positivity and growth in all the areas of the Bagua! When you know the location of your family's wealth and prosperity, health, or love area, you will have more control over these areas in your life. If your wealth and prosperity area is located in the spare room and that room is filled with all the clutter that would not fit into the rest of your home, what is that saying about your financial situation? Clean up that space immediately and see what happens to your wealth. If you, or your family members are prone to illness, check your Bagua grid, and find out what area of your home is in the family health and well-being. Assess that area. Is there clutter? Is it in a bathroom? What kind of items (artwork, furniture, etc) do you have displayed in that area? If nothing else, get rid of the clutter in the areas that you are most concerned about in your life right now. Move on to other areas to suit your priorities. As you can see, the Bagua grids are all intertwined. When each area is maintained nicely, the whole home functions better.

Ok, so go map your house, and let me know how it goes!

Just kidding! I think you will need a little more direction, and you know how I love to tell you what to do!

Here are my instructions to do a simple Bagua map on your own home.

You will need a blank piece of paper for this home-mapping exercise. Draw out a sample Bagua with just the titles of the centers on it, as illustrated below:

Wealth and Prosperity	Fame and Reputation	Love and Relationships
Family	Health and Well-Being	Creativity and Children
Knowledge and Wisdom	Career	Helpful People and Travel

To increase efficiency, I have a included the personal Bagua worksheet at **www.bethatmomnow.com**, so feel free to take a break and go print that out now.

Take your Bagua grid and hold it so you can read the words.

Make sure it is horizontal with the career Bagua up against your tummy. Stand outside your home and stand back from the front door so that you can assess where your front door is in relation to the rest of your home. Based on the length of your home, use the Bagua to figure out where your front door is located along the bottom edge of your Bagua Grid. Your front door will open into one of the following sections; Knowledge & Wisdom, Career, or Helpful People and Travel. If your front door is located directly in the middle of your home, the door will open into the **Career** center. If your door is located more to the left of your home, then it opens into the **Knowledge and Wisdom** center. Similarly, if the door is located more to the right side of your home, then your door will open into the **Helpful People and Travel** center.

Mark the location of your front door on your Bagua worksheet. You want to think of looking at your own home from a birds-eye view and lay the Bagua over top of it, using the front door as your starting point along the bottom of the grid. (See below for a completed sample)

Wealth and Prosperity Kitchen	Fame and Reputation Dining Room	Love and Relationships Bathroom
Family Sitting area with Fireplace	Health and Well-Being Stairs	Creativity and Children Bedroom
Knowledge and Wisdom Dining Room	Career Living Room	Helpful People and Travel Office

From the main front door, the room in the furthest left corner will be in your **Wealth and Prosperity** center. Similarly, the furthest right corner of your home from the main entrance door will be your **Love and Relationship** center. I know you can figure out the rest yourself. Add each room to your worksheet.

Use the main level of your home as a starting point. Once you understand how to use the Bagua, you can also apply it to other levels of your home, using the front door location as your starting point on each level. Each individual room can also be divided into the 9 areas of the Bagua, as well even smaller areas like your office desk.

To apply Feng Shui to your bedroom, for example, stand at the door looking inward. Using the Bagua grid, figure out where the door opens in relation to the whole room (left, right or center). The corner farthest left from the door is the wealth center in your bedroom and so on, according to the grid. The Bagua grid can similarly be applied to your desk area. When sitting at your desk, the corner of your desk to the far left of where you sit is your wealth center. Put a plant there for sure!

Now that you have mapped your home, it's time to start using the Bagua to help you bring everything you could ever want into your life.

As shown above, each Bagua grid area is associated with certain colors or elements (wealth and prosperity, for example, is represented by blue, purple and red, and by the element wood). You can "pump up" the positive energy in each center of the Bagua by displaying items with the corresponding colors or elements in these spaces. Take, for example, the wealth center: placing a red, wooden object in this area can increase the good energy here. This can be as simple as a plant in a red pot, or a piece of artwork with a wooden frame that features the color red . Always choose items that appeal to you personally. An item that is wooden and red that you find ugly will not generate positive energy. Always respect your own taste when decorating. As my mentor Michelle, from the East Coast Academy of Feng Shui says, "Your home does not have to look like a Chinese Restaurant" to have great Feng Shui!

By rearranging your home according to basic Feng Shui principles, you will significantly improve your life and realize all of your goals.

You don't have to be a Feng Shui expert to apply the principles of Feng Shui in your home. In actuality, it is incredibly simple to start applying the tips I have given you to create a more positively energized home.

Feng Shui can be simple when you apply the principles in logical, common sense ways in your home. I have armed you with a few basics, and now you are ready to start applying Feng Shui in every room in your house! Let's keep that positive energy flowing!

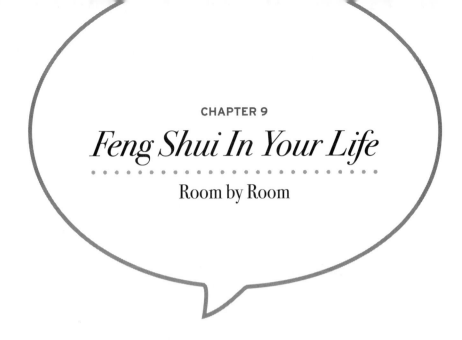

CHAPTER 9

Feng Shui In Your Life

· ·

Room by Room

"Your house is your home only when you feel
you have jurisdiction over the space."
– Joan Kron

Continuing on with our Feng Shui journey, let's take a look at some more practical and simple Feng Shui principles that you can start applying to specific rooms in your home.

With any room in your home, what you do there can have an interesting effect on the energy flow in those areas. Rooms that do not get used often have a stale, bland energy. Use the spaces you live in often and you'll get the positive energy moving in! Keep the function of each room in mind when you are creating the furniture flow and when you are considering what to keep in each room. Be sure that you use all of the things that you decide to keep in your home, or choose to get rid of them. The simpler you make your life, the easier it becomes to make it even better. An organized home is an efficient home and is a home where your entire family will thrive in. Let's get cooking!

Kitchen

The kitchen is said to be the heart of any home. It is in this space that the health of a family comes together. The kitchen should be treated with the respect it deserves, as it is your most important room in the house. Here are some clever Feng Shui ideas for your kitchen:

Keeping the kitchen in ready position makes it easy for anyone in the house to jump right in and get going with a meal.

Keep your kitchen in the "ready" position. Anytime you need to go into your kitchen to prepare a meal, or snack, or get a beverage, you should be welcomed into a space that is eagerly awaiting your next adventure together. The easiest way to keep your kitchen ready is to **clean as you go**. Put things away as soon as you are done using them and always clean up the kitchen when you are finished with a meal. This must also be a DO IT NOW project, and it is not one that you have to do on your own! Get everyone in your family helping. If you come home from work and you walk into your kitchen to prepare dinner and all of the dishes from last nights' dinner are still sitting in the sink, you are not going to feel very excited about preparing that meal. You might need some of those dirty dishes to prepare your meal, so you'll have to do those

dishes first. UGH. Double the work - added time to your meal prep
– reducing all efforts and efficiency in the kitchen. If all your dishes
are done and the counters are clear, you know that you will have
access to everything you need for taking care of that meal right
away. A clean kitchen feels amazing and will actually encourage you
to eat healthier. A clean kitchen says "Come on in and dine!", while
a messy kitchen screams "Honey, please pick up something on the
way home!"

As per my previously mentioned rule, everything in your
kitchen should have a space. Even a small kitchen can be efficient
if you follow this rule. When you can make time, go through all
of your cupboards in the kitchen and get rid of the things that you
do not use. If you haven't used an item in 3-6 months, it is probably safe to get rid of it. If the item is something you use 'once in
a blue moon' - like a punch bowl or 60 cup coffee maker- perhaps
there is a better place to store the item (the pantry, garage, downstairs storage) to free up some room in the kitchen? The kitchen
should be filled with things that you use regularly to prepare
meals and do baking. Everything else can be put somewhere else,
especially if you have a small kitchen. If you have nowhere else to
store it, you may just need to give that item away. Try to give the
item to a family member or a friend so that you know where it is
when you need to... um, borrow it. They'll store it for you — but
don't tell them I told you to do so!

Try to keep as much as you can off the counters and behind
closed doors. You want to have lots of room to work! Do your best
to stay in 'the power position' in your kitchen, whenever possible.
If your back is facing the entryway to your kitchen, (and you are
not prepared to renovate), you can use a mirror so that you can
see what's happening behind you. You don't want to be wondering
what your kids are up to while you're getting their meal prepared...
you want to KNOW!

Cupboards — Organize the cupboards in your kitchen by sorting things according to the use of each item.

If possible, try organizing and keeping all of the following things together in your kitchen.

- Things you eat on.
  - Plate, bowls
- Things you use for drinking.
  - Glasses, Mugs, wine glasses
- Things you cook with.
  - Pots and Pans
- Things you use for leftovers-
  - Reusable containers and lids.

  *This area can be frustrating to deal with. Here is my tried and true method: Stack the round containers together and stack all of the square and rectangular containers inside each other. Use one empty container to store all of the small lids, then organize the large lids together in a row and secure them using one of the containers as a "book end," as you would on a bookshelf. You can also use a pot lid-holder to store your reusable lids, as I do with my glass container lids. Only hold on to reusable containers that have a matching lid. This will put an end to the frustration of putting your leftovers in a container and then not being able to find the right topper!

- Things you bake with.
  - Cookie sheets, muffin tins, cooling racks. Usually, you can also store your cutting boards with these too.
- Things you clean with.
  - Kitchen towels and rags.
- Thinks you use to get the food to your mouth.
  - Spoons, knives, forks
- Things you stir and mix with.
  - Large stirring spoons, whisks, measuring cups and spoons
- Helpers.
  - Can openers, garlic presses, pizza cutters, cheese graters,
- Things you wrap with.
  - Parchment paper, aluminum foil, plastic reusable bags, paper lunch bags, plastic wrap.
- Things you need while cooking or baking.
  - Strainer, mixing bowls, casserole dishes, rolling pin.

Now... for the pantry. The pantry often makes us feel like we should be preparing for war, but let's face it... we never eat all of our pantry!

As one of your clutter clearing tasks, I want you to make the pantry a priority. Go set your timer and start taking everything out. Follow these easy steps to the pantry of your dreams!

1. Get a garbage bag, recycling bag and a donate bag ready.
2. Take everything out!
3. Manage and assess according to these rules:
   a. If the product is expired, throw it out and recycle the container. You may need to rinse first, depending what it is.
   b. If you will never use the product (be honest) and it is still good and has not been opened, donate it to your local food bank.
   c. If you will never use the product and it is opened, trash it.
   d. If you know your family will eat it, keep it!
4. Once you have your Keep it! pile, make things easier for you and your family by sorting your pantry items based on your use of the item. Here is one way to sort your pantry items:
   a. Spices
   b. Baking Goods-Flour, Sugar, Baking Soda, Baking Powder, cornmeal, chocolate chips, oatmeal, other grains
   c. Muffin tins, cake decorations, nuts, food coloring. (I have a Tupperware container that I use to store all of these little items in. Then, I know where they are when I need them.)
   d. Rice, pasta and beans
   e. Sauces, oils and vinegars
   f. Condiments
   g. Cookies, crackers, snacks and granola bars
   h. Cereals and instant oatmeal
   i. Cans of soup, vegetables and fruit,

Place everything back into the pantry and enjoy knowing exactly what is in there. It will now be easy to find anything. You will be able to train your family to put things where they belong (cereals go with the cereal, sugar goes with the baking stuff) and now anyone in your home can find the stuff to bake cookies easily.

And when it is not there?

How often do you find an empty box of crackers or granola bars in the pantry? It used to bug the heck out of me when that happened, but now I just allow for natural consequence to take over as the ultimate ruler. When you make the grocery list, do NOT shake all of the packages to see if they are empty or not. If a box in the pantry is empty, the item doesn't go on the list. If you happen to miss buying granola bars because an empty box was in the pantry and your granola bar lovers are upset that they won't have granola bars for a whole week, you now have an excellent opportunity to discuss the NEW grocery rule,

"If you finish it, YOU deal with the package and write it on the list."

Have a discussion with everyone in the household regarding them helping with the grocery order. You will now leave a grocery list in the kitchen somewhere accessible for everyone, along with a pen. When someone finishes the package, if they would like to see that item on the next grocery order, they must let the Galactic Overseer of the grocery world know that it was finished and we need more! Put some responsibility back onto your family to contribute to the Team. If they can't write yet, ask them to draw a picture, or ask you to add it to the list. Kids love to be involved, especially when it comes to their food.

Once you finish the pantry re-org, I would like you to move onto the fridge... *and then the freezer.* *groan* Using my rules from the pantry, apply them to these areas also. Your fridge will likely need a really good once over and then you will probably be able to maintain it on a weekly basis. Personally, I like to give my fridge a quick once over the night before grocery day. I get rid of any leftovers or wilted vegetables and make room for the new foods that are coming. When you are on top of your fridge, it will look tidy all the time and you will know exactly what is in there.

Tina's Tip: Use see-through leftover containers in your fridge so that you can SEE what you are keeping. If you can see that half an onion, you will be more likely to use it and not let it rot!

Dealing with Kitchen Refuse

The kitchen generates a lot of unusable products that need to be dealt with. Garbage gives off bad energy, so keep the effects to a minimum by keeping your garbage cans clean and hidden whenever possible.

While it is easy to treat all items as garbage, I would like to encourage you to think about everything you throw in the trash before you throw it away. We can be an incredibly wasteful society as a whole, and yet, if we each do a few things differently, we can keep an amazing amount of garbage out of the landfills. Choose to preserve space and the environment for our future generations!

In my opinion, waste produced in the kitchen is actually only composed of a few things:

- Organic Food Waste-Compostable
- Food Leftovers (with meat, oils, butters, etc.)-Garbage
- Dirty Tissues and Dirty Paper Towels-Garbage
- Empty plastic containers and bags, cans, cardboard, aluminum, glass jars, styrofoam containers (with the recyclable symbol). All of these items are recyclable.

If you composted and recycled everything possible in your kitchen, you could drastically reduce the amount of actual trash that you are sending out of your home every week! Our family of five routinely has less than 1 full bag of actual trash every week, 2 huge full bags of recycling, and 1 large bowl full of compost for the garden. I am extremely passionate about doing my part for the environment and I hope that I can encourage you to make a few small changes that can make a huge difference. Conserving the environment seems to be such a huge task; however, I believe that every piece of trash we keep out of the landfills and reuse is a step in the right direction. So, before you throw something in the garbage, ask yourself if it is really garbage. If you change, others will see your changes and may follow suit. Change the world one piece of "garbage" at a time!

Recycling requires maintenance. Often you will have to set up a location in your home to handle the recycling. Depending on where you live, you may have access to a recycling pick-up service that is included with your garbage. If you do not have recycling pick-up, consider signing up with an independent company that provides this service on a weekly basis. Typically, these companies charge a small fee (maybe $20 per month) to come and take away your recycling every week. In my mind, this is a small price to pay to do your part for the environment and it will save you the time of taking a trip to the depot every week or two. Your time is worth money…is it worth $20 a month to have someone else do that trip for you? If the $20 a month is too steep, or if this service is not available in your area, find a recycling depot close to your home where you can drop recyclables off yourself. Every time you recycle or compost, make sure you smile and appreciate the goodness of our earth. You are helping to turn things around!

Depending on your recycling system, you may be required to sort it into groups. If this is the case, set up a few bins inside of a closet close to the kitchen (where most your waste is produced). Label the bins, and then provide instructions to your family on what can go where.

As a Mom, you have the power to change the future by molding your children into responsible, caring environmentalists who have an appreciation for the world. Children quickly learn to rinse out yogurt containers and put them into the proper recycling bin if you provide guidance and positive reinforcement. **Be That Green MOM!**

Green Tip 1: Use Your Nose! Be cautious of things that have a strong smell. A lot of smells are not created naturally, so if something smells strong you can be assured that there are chemicals in it. Most of us have grown up to believe that the strong smell of cleaning products means things are clean and disinfected. In actuality, those strong smells are exposing you and your family to harmful chemicals every day! Just walking down the laundry and cleaning product aisle in any grocery store makes me feel sick. The smell test applies to everything, including cleaning and laundry products, perfumes, hair care and body care products (such as soap, cream, shampoo), candles, and air fresheners. Look at all of the products you currently use and read the ingredients. This is just as important as reading your food labels! Eliminate all products from your home that have chemicals in them. Choose natural or green cleaning products instead. These are better for you and your family, and in turn they are better for the environment.

Green Tip 2: Did you know that you can also make your OWN household cleaners? A little vinegar and baking soda combo cleans up sinks and tubs in a pinch! Your children will also love the chemical reaction these two ingredients make when used together — a NATURAL chemical reaction. Water infused with tea tree oil, lavender or eucalyptus in a spray bottle also makes a handy all purpose surface cleaner. These essential oils are naturally antiseptic... leaving your house germ free, at a fraction of the cost!

The Dining Room

Where you eat your food together as a family is a very important space in your home. For some families, dinner time is the only time of the day that they are together as a family. Make eating together at least once a day a priority. You play host to the most amazing guests every day — you and your family! Show yourself and your family how important eating is by setting the table nicely, using your good plates, some reusable cloth napkins, candles and flowers. This should be a peaceful room, free from any electronics. Soft music can be a nice touch as long as everyone can still hear each other. Focus on having good conversation during this important time. A good friend of mine, Joanna, gave me an interesting tip to help families talk to each other more at the table. Practice using BING!

B-ad

I-nteresting

N-ew

G-ood!

Everyone at the table has a chance to share about their day, using the letters of BING to help them along. It is an easy way to get people thinking and talking, and using different feelings to describe events and situations. It is amazing what you can learn about each other over a nice meal. Keep the lines of communication open and trusting with everyone in your family by encouraging this activity nightly.

Table Setting

Do not assume for one second that because you made the meal, you need to set the table yourself. Ask your children and husband to get involved in the table setting process — after all, they love to be included in helping out the family!

I often like to serve my food at the table, serving each dish into a reusable glass container with a lid. It looks much nicer than pots and pans, allows for everyone to 'help themselves', whilst keeping everyone seated together at the table. This also allows for EASY put away of leftovers and who doesn't like EASY?

Front Entries and Foyer's

This is the first area of the home that you and your guests see when entering the house. First impressions often say a lot about you, so make sure your entryway feels inviting, welcoming and warm! Your foyer is the gateway for all energy to arrive into your home, so it is extremely important that you take pride in maintaining this particular space. Make sure it is easy for anyone to walk up to your front door. Remove or prune back any bushes, trees or plants that might be blocking the way leading up to your door. Adding a plant or two outside the door of your home encourages the positive Chi energy to come in. (Fake plants will work if your climate cannot support real plants during some seasons.) Be sure to sweep and shovel too!

Ensure that the door functions well (handle works, door opens and closes properly, doorbell works), and that the actual door is clean and not in need of a paint job. Add a "welcome" sign or welcome mat for extra warmth. Incorporate the color red into your front entrance — you can paint the door red if you like, or just have some red in your welcome sign, mat, or door decoration (wreaths, door knockers, etc). The color red is said to attract wealth and prosperity energy into your home, so don't be afraid to experiment with this hue. Invite in that amazing life-filled energy at every opportunity!

How do you feel when you come home and walk in your front door? Take a moment to think about it. You may even choose to think about it the next time you walk into your home — what do you see? Are you greeted by a pile of cluttered shoes, jackets, a table full of unopened mail, flyers, and sunglasses? Is it easy to walk into your home, or do you have to squeeze through the door to get in because there are hockey bags and golf bags, or other "stuff" restricting you from opening the door? What colors do you see? Are they bright and cheery, warm and inviting, or cool and modern? What are some of the first things you see as you enter through the door, your favorite art pieces, a mirror, some plants?

Plants and flowers are an incredible way to say welcome as they encourage an abundance of positive energy. Use a variety of evergreens and potted flowers depending on your climate so that you always have some form of life at your front door.

How you feel at your front entry is what matters. You want to keep this area neat, clean, and uncluttered. : Shoes, jackets, hats and mitts should be stored away in closets with the doors closed, organized so they can be accessed easily. Try to make the flow into your home as smooth as possible; move furniture around so there is a nice clear path if you need to. Hanging pictures in the entrance area should make you feel peaceful and inspire you as you embark on every new adventure. Add plants, statues, decorative tables displaying cherished treasures or water features. You want to see positive things that you enjoy on your way in and out, and your guests will feel that positive energy too.

Things to Avoid: Avoid hanging mirrors directly across from the doorway, as this will reflect energy right back out the door. If your front entryway and your back entryway are directly in line with each other, the energy will come in one door and go straight out the other. This is not desirable and is difficult to change. If this is the case, add some plants or hang a wind chime or crystal in between the two doors to slow down the flow of energy and keep it within your home. If you have a staircase that leads straight up or down from one of your outside entrances, hang a wind chime or crystal in between the stairs and the door. This will slow the energy that would normally rush up or down the stairs and out of the home.

Bathrooms

As you can imagine, the bathroom generates a lot of negative energy. In addition, the flow of water out of your home in this area sucks positive energy down the drains of toilets, showers and sinks. If you want to improve your wealth and prosperity, use caution with the energy in your bathrooms. To keep the good stuff in your house, keep the toilet seats down and the shower curtains or doors closed. This may be a hard one for the kids (and others) in your life, but after a few gentle reminders everyone should be on board. It really is best to keep the bathroom doors closed at all times, but I find this often causes confusion about whether the area is already occupied.

Keep bathroom counter-tops as clear as possible, by putting everything you can away in cupboards or drawers. It sounds a little daunting, but again, if everything has a place, keeping it off the counter will be easy and will make you feel good. Add a plant or two to the bathroom, preferably close to the toilet. Plants help to absorb the negative energy that is generated in bathrooms. Plants are helpers

Adding a plant to your bathroom can really help reduce the negative energy that emanates from these areas.

at absorbing negative energy, so be sure to add one or two (near the toilet if possible).

Living Rooms

Living rooms are used for different things by different people. You may watch TV, visit with friends and family, or read in this spot. It may double as a play room or a workout room. No matter what you do in this room, make sure that there is positive energy flowing easily into this room. Try to set up the furniture so that you can easily walk into and around the room. Remove all clutter from this area and add plants strategically. If you have furniture in this room that cannot be pushed right up against a firm wall, you can use plants behind the furniture to provide grounding. As you likely entertain guests in this area try to set the seating up in a semi-circle, or full circle. That way, when seated, people are able to see each other. This will encourage good communication. If your living room doubles as a play area, workout center, or office, make sure there are bins or closets to store things away easily when you need the space for other things. Having a few organized bins or baskets to store toys in looks neat and is very easy for the kids to maintain on their own.

Baskets and Book Shelves can provide an easy way to keep toys in check in your living room area. Notice also in this living room that the oversized chair is not grounded by a back wall...a plant has been placed behind the chair to compensate.

Adult Bedrooms

Your bedroom is your sanctuary and is meant to rejuvenate, relax, and revitalize you. Bedrooms should be painted in calm hues and feel like an escape from all the uplifting energy in the rest of the home. When you enter your bedroom, you should immediately be calmed by the lack of stimulation in this area. Do not bring work into your bedroom — ever! It would be hard to let go of the day with a pile of work sitting next to the bed, so be sure to leave all gadgets/paperwork elsewhere in your house. Electronic items emit negative energy that may be harmful to your physical health. Keep only the book you are currently reading in your room, as a pile of books can be incredibly stimulating. Your side tables, dresser tops and tabletops in the bedroom should be free of clutter.

Aim to keep the floors clear in your bedroom. Dirty laundry gives off dirty energy, so be sure to store it in a basket or hamper in the closet, with the closet door shut.

Notice the calmness and duplicity in this bedroom, matching side tables, lamps and plants. Tidy and uncluttered. This is the kind of bedroom meant for relaxing and resting.

Avoid hanging mirrors in your bedroom, as they stir up too much energy!

Keep the alarm clock as far away from the bed as you can and get rid of the TV in your bedroom. If you insist on having a TV in your bedroom, enclose it in a cupboard with doors, or cover it with fabric before you go to sleep to reduce the energy impact.

Watching TV right before bed is extremely stimulating to the brain and can cause insomnia, bad dreams, worry, anxiety and general restlessness. This is not the kind of stimulation we want to encourage in our bedrooms. If you must watch TV before bed, turn the TV off half an hour before you go to sleep. Then proceed to follow your sleep routine...brush your teeth, wash your face and hop into bed with your book. Read for a minimum of 15 minutes before falling asleep, as this will distract your mind from the stimulation of the TV and your thoughts from the events of the day.

Turning the TV off a little earlier can also encourage some more positive stimulation in the bedroom. *wink wink* If you are relaxed and unstressed when you hit the bed at night, (and you can manage to keep your eyes open for 15 minutes before you fall asleep), the chance of a little hanky-panky increases! You will be surprised at the improvement in your mood!

If you are looking for someone to share your bedroom with, or you want to improve and strengthen your existing relationship with your bedroom partner, you can use Feng Shui in your bedroom to really get things moving in the right direction. Have pairs of things in your bedroom instead of single things. Place matching side tables with matching lamps on them on either side of your bed. Hang art that displays pairs of things. Have a pair of candles or a pair of chairs. Avoid cluttering up your bed with teddy bears or pillows, especially if you are trying to attract a bedroom mate. There needs to be room for two in your bed. Get rid of any items in your home that remind you of past romantic relationships, such as pictures of old lovers, or mementos that remind you of that relationship — Get rid of them! When you let go of these items, your mind will also let go and there will finally be room for exciting new love to enter. Let go of the past, and get excited about the future.

The placement of your bed can also be key to a peaceful, restful and healthy sleep. When you are lying in your bed, you should be able to see the door of the room just by lifting up your head. You want to be sleeping in the 'Power Position', so that you feel protected and relaxed. Avoid putting your bed in positions where you are in directly alignment with a door or window, as the stimulating energy flow may disrupt your sleep.

If you are standing at the door of your room, the best placement of your bed is with the headboard on the opposite wall, offset to one side of the door. The headboard should be up against a firm wall and there should be ample space to walk around either side of the bed. Do not push one side of your bed up against a wall. The energy needs to be able to flow around both sides and if you are sharing a bed with someone, both people should be able to easily get in and out of the bed as necessary without disturbing the other. Do not store items underneath your bed. Clutter under the bed is thought to be detrimental to your health and your finances, so move anything that is under there out immediately! If you have a bed with storage drawers underneath, it is imperative that you keep everything neatly folded and tidy.

When you get up in the morning, make your bed and open the curtains. A neat, bright, tidy room is a peaceful one, and just knowing that it is awaiting you at the end of the day will make you feel glorious.

Children's Bedrooms

As with your own bedroom, your children's rooms should be calm areas focused on resting — so no electronics in here either. Most children's rooms double as play areas, or homework space, and often there are a lot of toys, activities and books kept in a child's bedroom. The stimulating energy of toys and books can affect your child's ability to get a restful sleep. Allow them to keep one or two books, and try to house the rest somewhere else. If you choose to keep toys and books in your child's room, keep them in bins in the closet with the door closed, or in a toy chest. Homework should be stored in another area of the home, like an office, or out of sight in a drawer. Teddies and Lovie's also create that vibrant energy that we want to damper in the bedroom, so allow your kids a 1 or 2 favorites to sleep with, and let the rest of the teddies hang out at night for their teddy bear meeting in the closet. Use the "everything has a place" place rule to make it easy for your kids to keep their space neat, and they will learn to appreciate the effort required

Likewise, use warm, soft paint colors in your children's rooms. Ensure that your child's room is dark enough for good sleep, and feel free to leave their window open a crack to let in some fresh air. Keep the door closed when your child is sleeping to keep the calm energy in.

Without a closet organizer, we tried baskets to organize in Kayley's room, which did not work for us or her! Time for a little Tina loving!

I was determined to make this closet functional and practical for a growing young girl. I bought a new shelving unit and some baskets from Home Depot and I put it together myself. I was ready to get that closet under my spell!

Ahhh. Now that is a wonderfully organized closet suitable for play and easy to maintain for even a young child.

This photo is taken from the door of this room. Because of the window and the closets, the bed is in the best placement for energy flow (not in front of the door, the window, or the closet). This bedroom is painted a soft yellow, and there is little, or no clutter, and not a lot of visible toys or stimulating activities. The blinds are kept open during the day and the bed is made.

Place beds in the 'power position', ensuring the bed has space on both sides. Avoid storing items under the bed. Avoid using bunk beds from a safety perspective and from an energy perspective. The energy is not good for the sleeper on the top or the bottom.

Be good to your home and to your space. You deserve to be surrounded by beautiful things that make you feel happy and you should feel free to only surround yourself with these things. Make your shelter work for you and your family and you will protect yourselves from the elements, while thriving in the bounty of amazing energy.

Now that you've got your home working for you, it's time to get out of there and have a little fun with your family!

· ·

*"Being a single mom never gave Brooke
and I a lot of quality one on one time. Between
school, homework, work, her daddy visits, and
her hectic dance classes we always seemed to be
rushing from one place to another. We adopted
the 'Mommy and Me' personal day and I would
go into her room early in the morning, crawl into
bed with her and say "How would you like to
stay home from school today?" Brooke
and I would stay home from work and school,
and spent the whole day (sometimes even in our
PJ'S) doing whatever we wanted TOGETHER.
This quality mother/daughter time was
priceless and often looked back at
now with fond warm memories."*

— Krista O'Connor

· ·

CHAPTER 10
Family Fun Time!

. . . .

"In mere moments of togetherness,
families forge their most indelible memories."
– Wes Fessler

Being an innately responsible person, I have found that as I age, I have gotten more and more serious. I am a working woman and a mom. I need to keep my budget balanced, my house in order and be a good role model to my kids. I know that having fun keeps you young at any age, but I am a mom. I am supposed to be responsible, serious and firm... right?

In reality, I know I need to lighten up and have more fun — by myself and with my family. This life is to be enjoyed to the best of our capacities. As we age and get busier, we often put FUN on the backburner.

When I did my cross-Canada tour with my first book, Be That Girl, I had the pleasure of traveling with my cousin, Julie. Being away from our kids and being able to hang out together while traveling huge distances turned out to be a total blast. I don't think either of us had laughed that much in years! But it also turned out to be a total eye-opener. I remember Julie mentioning to me that she had forgotten how to have fun. And she's not the first mom that I have heard say this.

As moms, why do we let the fun parts of life slip away? Do we just not have the time for fun anymore with the demands that we place on ourselves with the responsibilities of work and family life?

True, once your children are grown and moved out of the house, there will be more time to have "grownup fun." But in the meantime, being "That Mom" means adding more fun and enjoyment to your family life. Believe me when I say that you are vibrant, adventurous, and creative — even if you have forgotten that you are! It is extremely valuable that you pass on these qualities to your children. When you rediscover those qualities in yourself, you will start being playful and joyous and laughing out loud again. Children are amazing at having fun and not taking life too seriously. So take a lesson from them and relax into the cool, fun-loving Mom that you are.

All work and no play makes for a dull life. If you force yourself to have fun with your children, you will find that you actually start having fun. Once you start having fun, you'll want more of it. Suddenly, more fun opportunities will start coming to you. How fun is that? The family that plays together stays together, so get outside and stick out your tongue to catch the raindrops, build sandcastles and Lego castles and block castles, play Barbies or Transformers, skip, run, do cartwheels and somersaults, and just laugh your head off for no real reason. I am counting on you to do this. You are "That Mom!

Time to Play — Think back to your own childhood and remember the things that brought you joy. For me, it was skipping — by myself, with a friend, or double-dutch with a group in the schoolyard. I loved skipping then, and I love skipping with my girls now! Take time to enjoy "kid" activities with your children. Engage in things that make you and your kids happy. After all, it's supposed to be fun!

It's also very important to go on fun outings with your kids. If you have more than one child, arrange to spend quality time away from the house with each of them separately. You don't have to be extravagant or break the bank. There are lots of fun and affordable things that you can do for an hour or two. Go to the local library or a bookstore where you can get a coffee and they can get a hot chocolate and then spend some time exploring new books together. Head to a play park and push them on the swings. Some fast food restaurants have play centers, so for the price of an ice tea and some french fries (or apple slices and yogurt if you prefer a healthier alternative), you can spend some time reading your book while your child screams and slides with the other little monkeys. Keep it simple.

When you have more than one child, it can be difficult to find the time to give them individual attention, especially when your kids are young. But even though it's hard, do what you can to spend time separately with each child. It is amazing how just half an hour together can impact your bonding and your communication. This is important at every stage and every age. You may have to bribe your teenager with shopping or food to get them to spend time with you, but do your best and make it a priority. You never know what you'll find out about them in those special moments. When it comes to teens, try to do something super fun, like rafting, or go-karting. Sharing these crazy adrenaline moments will increase your closeness and give you both an amazing memory that will never fade. Be that Crazy Mom!

Back on the home front, have a variety of creative activities on hand for your kids, things like coloring books, play dough, Lego, puzzles, games (individual and group), flashcards and books. Make these items accessible for the kids to help themselves. Children tend to get into mischief when they are bored. They will fight with each other or with you if their minds are not sufficiently occupied. As their mom, you cannot be expected to give them your undivided attention all day. In this case, use the "play-and-walk-away" technique (which I learned watching the TV show Supernanny).

First, help them choose an activity (like play dough, for example). Help them get it out and sit and play with them for a few minutes. Then you can get up and proceed with other things, such as household chores, or maybe taking a bit of time to relax. Use your evening TV-watching time to prep craft activities for the following day. Rent some craft books from the library, or search the Internet for ideas for cool, easy crafts. You do not have to break the bank when it comes to doing crafts and activities with your kids. It is amazing what fun things you can make with junk around the home, like toilet paper rolls, scraps of paper, or recyclables like cans and bottles. Be That "Green Mom" and use stuff you already have to make cool crafts with your kids.

Let them paint! I will admit that for some time, letting my kids paint at home gave me a mild panic attack at the thought of the resulting mess. But I've since gotten over my original misgivings. When properly supervised, painting is a fantastic activity both for you and for your child. Buy a "Splat Mat" — basically, it's a plastic sheet that you put on the table or painting surface so that the paint ends up on the mat and not your table (plastic tablecloths work well for this). Designate a few old shirts to be used for painting and crafting. I do NOT recommend using the "play and walk away" technique when your kids are painting! It doesn't take long for a painting disaster to arise, so this is one event where you will need to give your kids your undivided attention — don't learn this one the hard way!

Make your own play dough. There are a couple of great recipes for this fun and creative stuff on my website, **www.bethatmomnow. com**. Playing with something that you made yourself makes the journey just as much fun as the destination. Always enlist your kids to help with prep and clean up, even if they are just responsible for one thing. You can inspire a sense of belonging and camaraderie when you work together.

I encourage you to be in the moment and enjoy playing, or painting, or doing a puzzle or whatever else you are doing.

Let your kids each make their own playdough and let them choose what color they would like to use.

Making it is half the fun, and playing with it is awesome!

Your mind will have a tendency to wander while you are busy with an activity with your kids, and you will feel the pressure of unfinished household chores and other things on your to-do list. Instead, think of play like meditation. Focus on the task at hand and when other thoughts creep into your mind, acknowledge them, then simply let them pass. One way to be more present is to get involved yourself. When they're painting, grab a piece of paper and create your own masterpiece, or collaborate with your child on a shared masterpiece. Enjoy the moment, and do everything you can not to get distracted by the other things in your life. Taking just 20 minutes or so to enjoy an activity will be extremely pleasing for you and your children. They feel your energy and they know when you are happy, bored or distracted. When was the last time you just painted or played for 20 whole minutes?

There are lots of activities you can do that are fun and educational (multitasking at its finest!) As moms, we all want our children to be learning and expanding their minds whenever possible. An activity like planting seeds in the springtime teaches kids about how plants need water, sun, and time to grow, and allows them to watch how that happens over the course of the summer. Growing seeds that turn into vegetables and fruits is particularly exciting for kids these days. In North America, we are so far removed from the origin of our food. By helping your children learn where their food comes from you will be teaching them what it means to be self-sufficient. You will also be teaching them how to make healthy choices for their bodies by showing them real, natural foods

Doing simple science experiments at home is another amazing way to have fun and educate your children. It can be as basic as testing whether an object sinks or floats... and then asking: Why? All you need is a sink or tub full of water and some random objects. You can even make a boat out of a milk carton or other materials around the home that float. Be creative! As your kids get older, you can introduce them to more complex experiments, like that timeless classic, the "erupting volcano." How cool is it to watch the chemical reaction between vinegar and baking soda? I know that the thought of cleaning up the eruption is a little crazy...but it's FUN and it's SCIENCE, and I'll bet that your child will be eager to show their appreciation by helping you clean up.

The Internet is a wonderful source for science-related activities that are fun for the whole family (I recommend **www.sciencebob.com** if you're looking for cool experiments). Make time to search for activities to stimulate your science minds on a weekly basis. Letting your child be involved in the search for neat things to do is another way to spend time together and create some buzz around the upcoming activities. You will be helping your child learn how to use the Internet as a research tool and it will give you a plan. Be sure to let your child know that you will NOT be doing the activity right away. Kids are notoriously impatient, especially when it comes to fun. Train them to be patient, or at least give them a timeline for when you will be doing the activity with them. Planning ahead allows you to gather up all of the necessary supplies and set aside the proper amount of time for the activity. While there is something to be said for being spontaneous, using a little planning when it comes to this kind of fun can really increase everyone's enjoyment. And hey, if you enjoy it, you will look forward to the next activity. So, "plan it, then do it" when it comes to activities and everyone will be happier in the end.

A tough thing to do in this highly connected age is limit our kids' exposure to TV, computers, cellphones, iPods, tablets and other gadgets. Electronics give off negative energy (I'm fully aware that I'm saying this as I type on my laptop). That said, electronics are an integral part of modern life and you shouldn't worry about your kids adopting these technologies. They need them to survive in the real world. Just look at how teaching handwriting has now been replaced with iPad and laptop time in some schools.

At home, 30 minutes of screen time per day is ample for young kids (aside from watching movies). Using electronics is like going into a virtual world…one where the rules of life are very different. Whenever my girls turn off the electronics, I make a point of welcoming them back to the real world!

When your kids are online, direct them to interactive, educational sites. Make sure your children are in the same room as you when they are "surfing the net" so you can hear and see the sites they are visiting. There is so much easily accessible information online and searching for "bunny" can bring up some very interesting sites of the nature I'm sure you don't want your young impressionable children to see. Make use of parental controls to help restrict the kind of content that your kids can search for online, and keep your children close to you when they are surfing the net.

As a busy mom, it's easy to allow your children to spend time in front of electronics — I'll certainly admit to doing that from time to time. Even so, I try to be conscious of how much time they are spending staring at screens. When you don't use electronics as babysitters, you and your children are forced to find useful and fun things to do in the real world: going outdoors, reading, playing with toys (on their own or with you), playing games, going on adventures, taking walks together, going to the park, blowing bubbles, talking to each other, using your imaginations, doing crafts, cooking, baking... even writing books!

Do not be afraid to say "No!" to your children when they try to get you to let them watch more TV or stay on the computer past their allotted time. If you give in to their tantrums, you will see more tantrums — you can bet on that.

The Outside World — It's always a good idea to plan some outdoor time into your days, no matter what the weather. Kids are a lot more willing to go out in inclement weather than adults are. Fresh air is good for all of us, so if you schedule this into your day, it will be good for you as well as your children. As long as you all dress for the weather you will have a great time no matter what you do. Living in Western Canada, my family and I have certainly have seen our fair share of tough weather, but rain or snow, out we go! We sled and skate and make snow angels in the winter. In the fall, we rake leaves in the yard and collect leaves and berries for crafts. We jump in mud puddles, do sidewalk chalk drawings, and clean out the garden beds in the spring. In the summer, we

When you are dressed for the weather, you can have fun outdoors ANYTIME!

go biking, walking, swing on the swings and water the garden. By encouraging your children to be active, you will become more active yourself. Having children is a perfect excuse to have more fun outside all year round.

Go to the zoo or find other fun activities that can be done outside. It can be something as simple as going for a walk — even if it is just for five minutes. Just getting out of the house will energize you and your children. Holing yourself up inside will make you depressed and listless. The world is your oyster! Get out there and enjoy the pearls all around you!

Tips to make any day outing more enjoyable for everyone:

- Always pack a "Go Bag" when you head out of the house for an extended period of time. When the kids are old enough let them help you pack it. I always bring books, as well as crayons or markers and paper or coloring books. Sometimes we add toys to the Go Bag as well. If we are going somewhere for a large part of the day, I always pack their jammies and "attachments" (blankies and teddies). It's much nicer to fall asleep in the car on the way home when you have your jammies with you!

- One of my oldest friends (we first met back in kindergarten!) taught me this super-handy trick: Keep a pair of small, sharp, clean scissors in your "Go bag," diaper bag, or purse, which you can use to cut up spaghetti, dumplings, soup noodles, wontons, or any other food. It makes restaurant outings with young kids way easier.

- Bring healthy snacks and water for you and your kids. The easiest way to stay healthy is to keep healthy food with you at all times. Kids are notorious for being hungry all the time, so bring along age-appropriate snack foods that are easy to eat no matter where you end up. If you have more than one child, divide up the snacks in reusable containers so that each child has their own container (less mess, less fighting). Some good options are cut-up fruits and vegetables, crackers, dry cereal like cheerios, dried fruits, nuts (if there are no allergies), granola bars, cheeses and yogurt (just don't forget to bring a spoon). I like to bring food that my children (and I) can easily eat with our fingers and won't make too much of a mess. Have a large bottle or two of water with you at all times. Everyone needs to stay hydrated. You can also make a round of smoothies in the morning and then take them in "to-go" cups. Smoothies are extremely refreshing and nourishing and give you lots of energy to run after your kids. You'll need it, since they'll be running fast after having such a healthy snack.

- If you have younger children, it is a good idea to bring a stroller with you. Children tire more easily than you, and they (and you) will enjoy the flexibility of being able to be in or out of a stroller. This is one way to avoid the demands of "uppy, mommy, uppy" all day long. If you must succumb to the "uppies", having a sling will make it easier for you to carry your little bundle and still keep your hands free. Now that my kids are older, I find that I really miss the stroller! It was so nice to be able to store our things in the bottom of the stroller instead of carrying a big bag around. Once your kids outgrow the stroller you might graduate to a wagon, but eventually, you won't have that kind of rolling storage any more. Fortunately, by this time, your kids will be old enough to help you carry all the stuff.

- Be prepared for anything! You just never know where life will take you. Always pack sunscreen and sunhats and weather-appropriate attire. If it happens to rain on your parade, or your day at the zoo, having umbrellas, or at least jackets with hoods on hand means you won't have to cut your day short. If you have younger children, pack an extra set of clothes. Use a backpack. It will keep your hands free and it distributes weight more evenly. Even very young children can carry some of the stuff they need in their own backpack without too much complaining. Teamwork works, and, just as my mother taught me, it's never too soon to learn about personal responsibility (*"I am not your slave, Tina"* comes to mind here!)

Oh The Places You'll Go — Ryan and I have always been adventuresome and enjoyed traveling together. Once we started having kids, we wanted to make sure that we kept up our love of travel. We started taking Trinity camping with us when she was just a few months old, and we've never stopped. Ryan and I seemed to have a "thing" with camping on the May long weekend in Alberta. The nights get really cold in a tent, especially when it snows or pours rain the whole time, which means we end up getting really, *really* close to stay warm, and, well you can see where I'm going here. We've ended up with two babies born in February. So it seemed fitting that we would take Trinity camping with us in May, just after she was born.

It's my firm belief that if you can handle having a child at home, you can handle taking your child traveling. It is a bit challenging to pack everything that a baby requires, but with a portable play-pen and a few clothes, your baby will be happy no matter where you end up. All you need is LOVE (and a comfy bed).

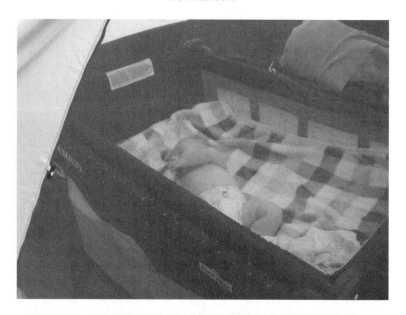

Camping can be a blast for you and your kids at any age. Be prepared with clothing for all weather and comfortable dry beds. Many memories can be made singing songs around the campfire!

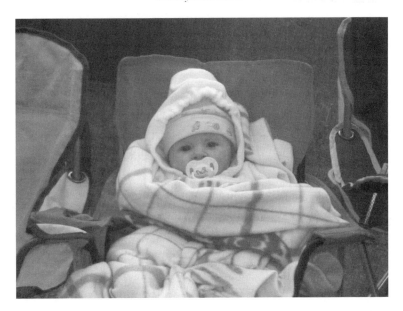

The first two years that Ryan and I had Trinity, we flew to British Columbia to visit my Dad and to Mexico for a resort vacation with my side of the family. I also took a trip with Trinity on my own to visit Ryan's sister and her family in Manitoba. For that trip, let's just say that I didn't exactly pack light. I can only imagine how crazy I looked trying to tote my baby and a *ginormous* (yes, that it is a word) cart laden with a car seat, playpen, stroller and luggage. I had Trinity in a "Baby Bjorn" carrier on my tummy and even though I was determined to do everything myself, I must have been putting out a bit of a "damsel in distress" vibe because so many people offered to help me throughout that whole trip. I was extremely impressed with how helpful people were!

When Ryan and I traveled to Mexico with Trinity she was just shy of being 12 months old. I made sure to bring some canned formula, as I wasn't sure that I would be able to find the foods we needed at the resort. The trip was a mini-reunion of sorts for my side of the family, so we requested an adjoining room with my dad. Since my dad likes to wake up with the sun and go to bed early, he didn't mind staying back and reading a book while Ryan and I ventured out to enjoy the nightlife at the resort with my brother and my sister. Ah, freedom! Even if you're on your own, having an adjoining room, or at least a separated bedroom area, is my recommendation for any young family. Young kids inevitably need more sleep that you do, so it's great to be able to put them to bed in one room, then you and your partner can have some time alone to hang out in your hotel bed and watch TV or cuddle in the hammock while your children get their *zzz*'s.

It was a bit frustrating to be on vacation with a child that still takes daily naps, especially being there with my siblings, who had no children and, as a result, had complete freedom with their days. Once or twice a day, Ryan and I were forced to go back to our room and either nap or read while Trinity napped (I know... sounds tough, right?). There were also a lot of beach naps for little Trinity. I will never forget how she took her first few steps on a sandy beach with bare feet...she hated it!

A few years later, my family decided to do another trip to Mexico. At that point, Ryan and I had three young daughters, so we decided to bring along our 16-year-old niece, Brooke, to help us out with the girls. Brooke has always been like a daughter to

A nap on the beach is just as good as a nap in your own bed. Don't be afraid to let your children have fun in new places!

Trinity and I both loved the afternoon hammock naps that a tropical destination afforded us!

us, and we figured that the extra cost of bringing her with us to the all-inclusive resort was a small price to pay to spend some extra time with her, and get some much-needed relax time in the evenings with the rest of my family. Let me tell you, that was luxury traveling at its finest! Brooke was an immense help and we all had a blast!

Contrary to what you might think, flying with children is not bad at all — as long as you can get them the sleep and food they need. Keep your carry-on bag stocked with emergency granola bars or crackers so your kids won't "die of starvation," and do your best to pick flight times that are not too late for your little ones. On the flight back from our first trip to Mexico, we ended up flying very late at night. Poor Trinity was so overtired, and had such a hard time falling asleep on the plane, that she ended up crying almost the entire time. My adrenaline was racing the whole time, and I'm sure that the other passengers on that night flight wanted to toss Trinity and I out with a parachute so they could get

With three little girls in tow, it was awesome to have my niece, Brooke, as my sidekick. A good sling, a stroller and a backpack or two are key items when you travel with little ones.

Kayley looks like she is really reading my book too! Afternoon rest periods are the best when you are on vacation. Strive to get this kind of rest when you are at home too!

A large group of us traveled to Mexico as a way to spend some real quality family time together. Notice in this picture that almost all of us are signing "I Love You!" How fitting!

Our first big trip as a family of 5. With some careful planning, a young family can have blast traveling the world!

some sleep. So make an effort to fly during decent times for the good of you, your baby, and the other passengers. If you end up having a horrible flight, be kind enough to yourself to let go of it and not worry about it. Most likely, the vacation was worth the bad flight and at least the other passengers will have something to talk about the next time they find themselves in a discussion about "nightmare flight experiences."

If you're financial situation right now means air travel is out of the question, it doesn't mean you can't get out and explore the world as a family in other ways. Take a road trip to a cool town near by, or you can always go camping!

Happy Campers — I am a big fan of camping and endorse it whole-heartedly. It doesn't cost much (for the actual campsite), but it's hugely enjoyable for everyone. Getting out there into nature and back to basics is more important than ever in this day and age, where our days are packed with activities and we're "wired" to the max. If yours is like most families, then there's a good chance that both parents are working, "free time" when the kids aren't in school is spent doing activities like hockey, swimming, music lessons, dance, soccer, tutoring, homework, reading exercises, yard work... the list goes on. The more "connected" we are with the world via our laptops, cellphones and tablet computers, the less time we spend actually communicating with each other. Sometimes it feels like we're living in a virtual world. Camping is a way to enjoy the real world.

It doesn't matter whether you camp with a tent, a holiday trailer, an R.V., or you rent a rustic little cabin. The point is to try living without many of the luxuries that we are accustomed to having. Cooking food on a camp stove (or over a campfire) takes more effort, but that effort makes it taste so good! Depending how you camp, you may not even have easy access to running water. Suddenly, you're washing your hands from a jug or stream and boiling water to wash dishes. Living without luxuries and

The family that camps together, stays together! Be adventurous as a family when you are camping. We love to find cool, lazy rivers that you can raft down on a hot, camping day. Use umbrellas, hats and sun-suits to protect your family from the elements while you play in the sun.

By the time we had Payton, I was ready to say goodbye to the tent and hello to the tent trailer. What I love about the tent trailer? It sleeps all of us comfortably off the ground, it has heat, yet it still feels and sounds like you are sleeping in a tent. When you have children, a dry, warm sleeping area is essential when you are camping.

Even the girls enjoy relaxing in a hammock once in a while when we are camping. When you're camping, life slows down a little and everyone is just more relaxed. Notice Trinity's "I love you" sign. You should all know how to sign "I love you" by the end of the book...there will be a test!

modern conveniences really makes you appreciate what you have at home. It also builds confidence by showing you that your family can make do with much less than what you have.

Make a conscious effort to leave all electronics at home when you go camping. Imagine a weekend (or a week!) without TV or cell phones, iPads or computers. What would you do to fill your time? Well... you could fill your days with fishing, hiking or walking. You could teach your kids emergency skills such as how to make a fire or how to make a rainproof shelter with tarps. You could play cards or a board game, go swimming or boating, go to a park, go for ice cream, fly kites, build sandcastles, sing songs around the campfire, tell ghost stories... You have nothing but time! It is amazing how the dynamics of a family change when you change the surroundings.

Once the kids go to bed (that's to say, if they end up going to bed before you do), then you and your partner can sit around the campfire and talk — about your day, about your future. When you remove yourselves from your day-to-day routine, away from work and chores, it becomes easier to let yourself dream. Remember, you can make your life whatever you want it to be. Vacations are the perfect time to envision a new future (I am sure you will want to add "more family vacations" to that future).

Tips for overnight travel with kids

- For air travel, pack one bag of checked luggage per kid, and carry on a backpack. If your kids can manage, have them carry on a small bag with a few of their things in it (a stuffie, a blankie, some coloring stuff or a book). Remember, you may end up carrying your child's bag, so keep that in mind when you decide what to put in it. On most airlines, for the first two years, kids fly free, so use this opportunity to do some air travel with them because it will never be cheaper than that! Babies are very easy to travel with and the earlier you travel with your kids, the more experienced you will all become at enjoying new places.
- Pack a laundry bag to keep everyone's dirty clothes separate from clean clothes. If you each have your own laundry bag (something as simple as a pillow case), then, logically, at the end of the trip your clothes will all fit back into your own suitcases. When you get home, all laundry bags go into the laundry hamper, while the rest of the items get put away – *badda bing, badda boom*! So easy! You can teach your kids to put dirty items in their own laundry bag at a very early age. Kids love to be helpful and praised. It's a great way to ensure clean clothes stay clean and dirty clothes stay off the floor for the duration of the trip. Imagine how neat your hotel room will look, and feel!
- When visiting foreign countries, let go of your anxiety. You may feel that you need to pack *everything*: the stroller, the playpen, the car seat, the high chair, the kitchen sink...). Do some research beforehand. Perhaps you can rent a car seat from a car-rental company? Do you even need a car seat if you're just going to be taking taxi's or buses for the most part? Depending where you are staying, you may have access to things like high chairs,

cribs and strollers, so check before you go to eliminate the need to bring extra things. If you are going to visit family, see if they know someone who can lend you some of their things while you're there. If you're staying with close friends or relatives that you'll be visiting often, perhaps they will want to purchase some of the items you'll need from a thrift store or consignment store. Even if you know you'll never be back, you can always donate the items to a local charity, or family in need, or even sell it back to the consignment store. Either way, it may be cheaper and easier to buy some second-hand items than it is to pay the extra/oversized luggage fees. The less you have with you when traveling, the easier it will be. Easy is good!

- If you are going to a country that is poorer than the one you live in, plan to leave some of your clothes and your kids' clothes and coloring books there for a family in need. I have been fortunate to be given hand-me-down clothes for my children, and my mother-in-law, Charlene, keeps my kids well stocked with clothes from the second-hand stores, so, I definitely don't mind leaving behind a few outfits for someone else. I love leaving books as well; literacy is so important. You can ask around as to whether or not there is a charity that will receive your donations, or just approach a local family on your last day and offer them the items. Share your abundance with others. It feels amazing!

- Find out in advance if there are vaccinations recommended for your travel destination. Most major cities have a travel clinic where they will advise you on what you need and administer the vaccines. Look into natural alternatives to protect yourself when you travel. Homeopathic remedies and vitamins can be used as natural mosquito repellants, as well as vaccinations for certain conditions – no shots needed! Visit your local homeopath, naturopath, or health-food market for more information. There is also a smorgasbord of information online in regards to travel (though be aware that not all of it can be trusted). In any case, be prepared.

- Make sure everyone in your family has a valid passport. Your children's passports need to be renewed more frequently than yours, so check the expiry dates regularly. Being "That Mom" means being prepared for anything. You never know when you might need to travel to an exotic location with your family at the last minute!

- Bring along extra sunscreen. Sunscreen can be extremely expensive in foreign destinations and may be hard to find depending on where you go. I highly recommend purchasing sun suits, or rash-guard shirts, for your kids and yourself. Sun suits are one-piece rompers that cover three-quarters of the child's arms and legs and are a good thing for young kids. Rash guards are t-shirt or long-sleeve shirts used by surfers to protect their torsos while they're paddling. The material used to make sun suits and rash guards usually has a UV protectant rate of 50 to 100, plus, it can't rub off the way sunscreen does. Your kids can throw these items on easily during the day and with a little sunscreen on their legs and forearms, they're ready to hit the beach! The material dries really quickly too, and the surfer look is really cute and stylish, so even fashion-obsessed 'tweens won't mind wearing them.

Oh The Places You'll Go (Without The Kids...) — While I am an advocate of family travel, I am also a firm believer that as "That Mom," you are entitled to vacations without your kids. As a first-time parent, it can be extremely difficult to pull yourself away from your baby for a night. You might feel like no one will be able to take care of your baby in the exact way that you want. Perhaps you feel you are being selfish to want time away from your children. Perhaps there's no one close by who you would feel comfortable asking to take care of your child for an extended period of time. We are so blessed to have family around to help us with our girls. If you don't enjoy that same luxury, it is worth it to find a reliable babysitter. If you are strapped for cash, talk to other moms about childcare swapping arrangements where they look after your children one night, and you look after their children on a different night. It's worth it!

Whatever is keeping you from parting with your child for one night, or 10, I officially give you permission to let it go! You deserve some "adult time." A quick overnight at a spot not too far away can really help you get back in touch with yourself. If you are married, this overnight can be a re-kindling of your affections. Nothing adds heat to the fire of your marriage like an overnight in a hotel without kids! You can be loud and crazy and free to be yourselves. You don't even have to leave your town or city — just rent a hotel room right in town and find someone to watch the kids for the night. Pretend you're a brand new couple again and enjoy spending that time together.

After we had Trinity, Ryan and I took our first overnight adventure to Banff, which is just a short drive away from Calgary. Since then, we have made going to Banff a yearly tradition. Sure, we were nervous that first time. We left Trinity in the capable hands of Ryan's parents — a nurse and a teacher — but still, the whole hour drive, I worried about all of the things that might or could happen, all the "What ifs…" But as Ryan and I settled into our hotel and breathed in the fresh mountain air, I began to remember what it was like to be Tina again. By the time we were in the outdoor hot tub, I had a smile on my face and not a care in the world.

Since then, we have become addicted to traveling together, without our kids. The time Ryan and I spend together at home is often at the end of the workday when we are too tired to really focus on each other. When we are away from the kids, it's just us again. For our 10-year anniversary, Ryan and I took our first European vacation to Italy for almost three weeks, without our kids. I'm not going to mince words here; it was the trip of a lifetime. Ryan and I rode trains, got lost, took a gondola ride, ate olives, chocolate, bread and wine on a huge rock while the ocean waves crashed in front of us and added our lock to lovers' lane.

The history, the scenery and the company made us fall in love all over again.

We learned a lot, we laughed a lot, and we fell in love all over again. We missed our children every day and on the flight home I had butterflies in my tummy from the excitement and longing to hug my sweet babies again. As much as I appreciate traveling with Ryan, our family thrives when we're all together.

If you are a single mom, or with someone who doesn't enjoy traveling, consider going on a scrapbook weekend, or plan a spa getaway with a friend or two. Or just rent a hotel room for yourself and read a book and have baths and order room service for a whole day. Any way you can remove yourself from the routine where you do everything and find some time to focus on you is worth the effort.

YOU! Remember 'That Girl'? The one you used to be…before you had kids? You've forgotten about 'That Girl' for long enough. It's time to Release your Inner Girl, Mommy!

"*Stay true to yourself. You don't have to give up your own passions and interests once you become a mom. It's important that you find time for what you love to do. Reading, writing, exercising — make these a priority and find a way to incorporate those into your routine. Easier said than done, I know, but you should at least aim to keep doing what you love, even if you don't get to do it as often. If you take care of your own needs, you will be happier and will function better as a mom.*"

— *Catherine J. Gillis*

CHAPTER 11

Release Your Inner Girl!

· ·

"You yourself, as much as anybody in the entire universe,
deserve your love & affection."
– Buddha

I know you love your family and your family loves you! Now I want to talk a little more about self-love. The way you treat yourself will have a direct impact on how you feel. How you feel about yourself will have a direct impact on how others treat you. When you are confident, bold, and smiling, you will attract helpful, amazing people to you, and they will treat you with the respect that you deserve when you are in that state. When you love yourself, others will be attracted to you and will find it easy to love you.

Now I want you to think about ways that you show yourself that you love YOU. How do you say "I love you" to yourself? I want you to ask yourself that question right now and see what you come up with. What do you do for yourself that says... "I Love YOU!" "I am Important" "I deserve this" ? Get out your journal, or use the pages in the back of this book, to write "How do I show myself love?" and then jot down some answers.

What did you think of when I asked you how you show yourself love? I hope that you came up with a long list of things that you do just for you. If you couldn't even write one thing down, don't worry. That won't happen anymore. I got you covered from here on out!

You need to Love Yourself First. Or, as one of my friends Neelam would say, you need to **F-L-Y... First Love Yourself!**

Time to stop thinking like a Mom, and start thinking like a GIRL. You started off as a girl, and you're STILL a girl, and it's time to put you first. I want you to make the time to put some of these things into your life right away. YOU deserve to be recognized, to be pampered, be loved, and be happy. Did you know that you could be the one who does all that for YOU?

How do you love yourself? Let me help you count the ways...

Cleanliness is next to godliness...

Ok, Mom. Taking a shower or a bath daily should not constitute personal time. It should be looked at as a given, like using the washroom. Use your personal time for other things and make showering and bathing a mandatory event that you give yourself permission to take daily if you want to, without guilt!

Preparing yourself for the day and being ready for anything, does take some preparation. As a mom, it may take extra planning. You may have to get up earlier, or stay up later. Whether you are an evening bather or enjoy a morning shower, make time every day to cleanse your body. When you are clean, you subconsciously feel better about yourself. Keep your body smooth and silky by removing unwanted hair from wherever you like, and apply cream or oil immediately when you get out of the shower or bath.

Keep your nails (feet and hands) trimmed, clean and filed. Treat yourself to a manicure or pedicure at a local nail salon once in a while, or do your own at home. Be sure to remove the polish as soon as it starts chipping or peeling.

Brush your teeth at least twice a day, if not more, and be sure to floss your teeth at least once per day. Visit the dentist yearly to keep up with those healthy teeth! Dental hygiene can have a serious impact on your relationships and your appearance in the long run, so take the time to keep your teeth shiny and your breath fresh!

Lingerie

Ladies, now is the time to remember that, mom aside, you are still a girl with needs... pretty, exciting needs. Loving yourself includes treating yourself to things that make you feel good all over! No matter what relationship you are in, or not in, I am a firm believer that you need to prioritize your undergarments! The most excellent thing about lingerie is that for the most part, no one else knows you are wearing it. But you do...and that is what really matters!

The way we feel about ourselves is all in our heads and when we treat ourselves well, we will be more apt to act like sexy goddesses. When we feel sexy and attractive, we are more likely to act more confidently, and feel better about ourselves and our bodies. We will also be more willing to put ourselves out there as the women we are! You may chastise sexy lingerie, claiming that you are doing it all for the men, or that it's degrading, dirty, or uncomfortable. But that's all in your heads ladies, and it's time to change that stinkin' thinkin'!

In his painting titled 'Hang to Dry', artist Troy Aitken reminds us to take care of our lingerie!

Your undergarments are the first thing you put on every day. What does your lingerie say to you right now? Do you feel "ready for anything" with your undies? Starting your day with pretty coordinating bras and panties can change the way you feel about yourself. Try to buy pretty, lacy things that are still comfortable and functional and that make you feel feminine, or sexy. It is a fine balance and one worth putting the effort into. Bras and panties are not cheap, but they are worth budgeting for. Make sure you are wearing a bra that fits you well. You want the "girls" to be nicely lifted and looking perky, while providing the support you need all around. Boutique lingerie stores may be expensive, but the staff are generally extremely knowledgeable and you can get a really decent bra fitting done for you. Different bras fit differently, so do your diligence and get what you want out of your bra. Once you find one that you love, get one in black, cream and white!

If you care for your lingerie by washing gently and hanging to dry, your lingerie will last. Remember also that sexy matching bras and panties can really heat things up in your bedroom when you add a little confidence and a pair of heels!

If you can get the nerve and the confidence, try using "costumes", or other forms of lingerie in the bedroom as a way to spice up your bedroom life. Believe me, as a mom of three, I know what it's like to try and fit "sex" into your already busy life. I think it is an important part of our womanhood, and one that we should feel good about putting priority on.

How exciting to start your day with lingerie! Now what are you going to put on over top of those pretty little numbers? You need to start dressing like the person you aspire to be right now... successful, amazing, put together, stylish, couture, fit, fabulous, flirty, fantastic, fun, business, classy, or casual. However you see your ideal you, it's time to start dressing the part, and Fake it 'til ya make it!

Dress for success

What you portray to others is based on how you see yourself. How do you want others to respond to you? What do you want your style to say about you? I want to encourage you to embrace your own style, and start rocking it! Be yourself and have a little fun with your wardrobe. As mom's, our bodies have undergone some amazing changes over our lifetime. Let me tell you something ladies, it's not the size the matters, it is the confidence you have in your own body that really matters. Who cares what your body looks like? The only opinion that should matter to you is your own. If you are not happy with your body no matter what shape or size it is, you are going to emanate that to others and they will respond to that energy. If you are confident in yourself, you will immediately become attractive, sexy, and interesting to

Ladies, I am giving you permission to have a little fun with your wardrobe. Accessories keep your outfits fresh, fun and exciting and allow you to change your style to suit every occasion. Check out the black shoes in this picture...one with the sparkly boot belt and the other with the zip on fur... same shoes, so many options! Belts, hats, wraps, jewelry, shoes, purses... add some pizzazz to your day with accessories!

everyone no matter what your body looks like. Your self-loving energy will draw other self- loving people to you, and vice versa.

One way to "love the skin you're in" is to dress in clothing that accentuates your style and your personality. As moms, we are used to being "in between" sizes when it comes to clothes. At every stage of your weight losses and gains, dress yourself in clothes that fit your body well, or add shape, to your body. Wearing frumpy clothing that is too big for you, or clothing that is just plain too tight for you, is not doing you any favors, and is likely not that comfortable. Love your curves, or lack of curves, and dress them appropriately. Choose designs that you like and styles that you like, and be sure you are portraying the image that you want to the public. With the clothes you wear, you are sending a signal not only to others, but to yourself, about the person that you are. Your clothes are an external reflection of how you feel about yourself. There are days when you'll dress casually in sweats, or for the runway, or just for a business meeting, but be sure you feel good in each outfit.

If you are still rockin' your maternity jeans a year after delivering your baby, it's time treat yourself to some new big girl clothes. Trading in those nursing tops in for shirts that don't have such easy access can make you feel like a woman again!

Clothes are a huge expense no matter what you do for a career. Just as you would shop for your children a few times per year for back to school, or as they grow out of their clothes, you also need to do the same for yourself. At least yearly, assess your wardrobe and get rid of items that you no longer wear due to size, style, or fit. Donate your clothes to others, or find a second hand or consignment store to sell your used clothes to. Second Hand stores are an amazing way to keep your wardrobe refreshed all year long at a fraction of the cost of new clothes, so use your clothing budget wisely by shopping second hand. Even if you have an unlimited clothing budget (lucky you), consider shopping second hand for the environment! Reduce, Reuse and Recycle even with clothing! I have a favorite consignment store that I shop at in Calgary. They specialize in brand name, quality ladies clothing. I have such great success at this store for everything from jeans, dress pants, shirts, tunics, dresses, shoes, purses and accessories, that I rarely step into a mall for clothes. I love finding the perfect pair of jeans, already nicely worn in and hemmed just to my size at the consignment store…obviously there is another amazing girl out there that is just my style and my size…and to her I say "Thanks"!

At the mall, you will be bombarded with all the latest fashions and fads, which is awesome if those styles work for you. The thing I love about consignment shopping is the flexibility of styles in the clothing. Consignment stores offer a wider range of styles and options than what you might find at the mall at any one time. One of a kinds and rare little treasures can be exciting to find. On the down side, that perfect dress that you just found on the shelf at the consignment store may be just a little big, or just a little small, and there is no other size. At consignment, you can only wear the "shoe" if it fits!

Invest in a few key pieces of clothing that can be mixed and matched, like a red skirt, black jacket, red jacket, black pants, white shirt, black shirt. Just imagine the possibilities with those items! You can easily add items to that wardrobe over time, and you will increase your wardrobe potential. Buy colors that you look and feel good in.

Once you get those few key outfits, you can mix and match all week long, as long as you add some pizzazz! One way to keep your clothing exciting on a budget is to SUCCESSORIZE…use accessories to add some WABANG! And SHEZAM! to your day.

You want, and NEED, to get noticed, whether you think you do or not. You NEED to get noticed in all the right ways! An easy, and affordable, way to do that is with accessories.

Here are a few accessories that can take your outfits to new heights!

- **Belts!** Big, fat colorful ones, wide, soft embroidered ones, skinny leather ones, huge cowgirl buckle ones! Belts can be worn high up just below the ribs, low down and to the side, or right around your waist. You can use soft scarves as belts also to mix up the material and add softness to an outfit.
- **Flowers!** I love to add flowers (fake or real) to my outfits. A flower in your hair, a flower pinned on your shirt, or a flower pinned to your purse. So girly, fun and summery.
- **Jewelry!** Earrings, bracelets, necklaces, watches, fashion glasses. You can change the style of an outfit based on the jewelry you pair with it. Try to have a mix of elegant, chic and casual jewelry.
- **Shoes!** Need I say any more? The right shoes can make an outfit. If you're like me, sometimes the outfit starts with the shoes, and then you have to find the right clothes to wear with them. No matter what you wear on your feet, make sure your shoes are comfortable, or at least bearable for the amount of time that you'll have to wear them. Shoes can be another one of those expensive items, but you only need a few pairs of the right shoes to make your outfits shine. Take good care of your shoes. The more pairs you have, the less wear each pair will take. If you need to use that as an excuse to buy more shoes, go for it, but don't blame me.
- **Shoelery!** Yeah, that's right. Jewelry for your shoes. We're talking Bling baby. This is an amazing way to change one pair of shoes into 3 or more! With a couple pairs of Shoelery, you can clip on and off the style that you need to suit a variety of outfits. This is great for when you are traveling and need to create some shoe variety with limited space, or if you want to jazz up your favorite pumps for a wedding or special event. I love the boot jewelry and the zip on fur...instant "boots with the fur" for when you need it.

- **Purses, and clutches!** Again, you need a variety of styles of purses to go with your wardrobe, but if you select 3 great bags of different styles that will mix and match with your wardrobe, you'll be laughing. An oversized brown bag, a tiny silver clutch, and a medium size black purse are all you might need. Adding colored purses can really make your outfit pop, so add to your collection when it becomes a priority. No matter what purse you are using, make sure you keep it clean and tidy, just like your home. Be sure to empty your purse of gum wrappers, receipts and anything else you don't need on a daily basis. The less you keep in your purse, the better your back and shoulders will feel and the easier it will be to find the things you need when you need them. For awesome purse organization and easy purse swapping, buy yourself one or two small cosmetic bags and sort your purse goodies into these bags. Chapstick, lipstick, personal monthly items, nail file, Band-Aids, allergy pills, business cards, etc. Use a red wallet! The color red attracts wealth and prosperity into your life, and red wallets just look awesome. Mirrors multiply energy, so if you have one in your wallet, keep your debit cards and cash by the mirror, and DO NOT keep your credit cards by the mirror. You don't want to increase your debt!

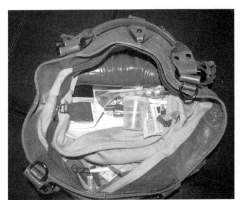

This very messy purse is how most of our purses look! With no organization, the things you need to carry with you daily can really start piling up.

My first rule with any organizing project – "Take Everything Out!"

Sort everything in your purse. Garbage?
Keep it?

Keep all of your "personal" items in one bag...
makeup, perfume, monthly business items, nail
files, etc.

Keep your business, or stationary needs
in this organizer. Your business cards, a pen,
and all of those reward cards that you have
been collecting.

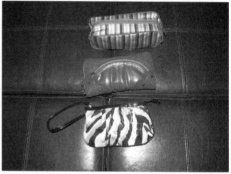

Once everything is organized into a container,
it will make it easier for you to swap out purses
without leaving anything behind, and it will make
it easier for you (and others) to find things.

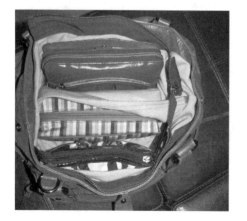

Ahhh. All Done. What a nice clean
purse you have? The better to grow
your wealth with, my dear!

- **Hair!** Clip in highlights of bright colors, use cute barrettes and sparkly headbands, and don't be afraid to exercise your own style. Your hair is a reflection of you, be creative and fun, but make sure that your hairstyle is functional for you. Mom's need hair styles that are easy to maintain, cute, fun, and stylish. A great hairdresser can help you find an amazing style to suit you and your lifestyle.
- **Fascinators!** Like a headband, with a big, vibrant flower, feathers or plume to one side. Very British and Eye-Catching (Fascinating!).
- **Hats!** I love hats of all kinds. We all need the bad hair day hat, but I want you to have a couple amazing hats that you wear to feel good, instead of trying to hide! There is at least one hat out there for everyone, but you have to take the time to try them on to find one. Careful, a love of hats can turn into an addiction!
- **Scarves!** Keep a variety of scarves on hand for different occasions. Scarves can provide the added warmth you might need when the weather is cold, and they can also be used to beautify outfits. From silky and smooth, to wooly and warm, and in all kinds of colors, scarves are a fun way to add color, texture, and warmth to your outfits.
- **Wraps!** When it's not cold enough for a jacket, but too chilly for just a tee, you need to have your wrap in tow! Wraps are similar to scarves, but they often provide a lot more coverage and warmth. As with scarves, wraps can be worn in a variety of ways that can make your outfits go farther, especially when you are travelling. I hate being chilly, so having a wrap neatly folded in my purse at all times is a great way to ensure that I will always have a warm buddy.
- **Tights!** Fun, colorful, patterned tights have become super popular, and why not! Super high socks, bright tights and leggings are a comfortable, stylish option for wearing underneath tunics and dresses. Not sure how you feel about nylons, but I will do whatever it takes to never have to squeeze myself into a pair of them again.

If you feel great in what you are wearing, you will look great to everyone else. So just go for it when it comes to your style and your brand. Express yourself with your clothes, and don't be shy about letting your clothes accentuate your body. You are amazing just the way you are. Love yourself by letting the real you come out and be shared with the world!

You're never fully dressed without a smile.

Now that you're dressed, make sure you finish yourself off with your dazzling smile. Really, you should already have that smile on your face as soon as you wake up, but at least try to have it on by the time you are finished getting dressed. When you smile, it makes you feel good. Which makes others around you feel good, and it attracts positivity to you. Try to smile all the time, even when you don't want to...especially when you don't want to. Turning that frown upside down can have an immediate impact on your frame of mind. Remember that your appearance is a reflection of how you feel about yourself. Your smile can change the world.

My sister-in-law Krista clearly knows how to add a smile to her day!
Add your smile every day to increase your happiness.

Flowers are an amazing way to add positivity and energy to your day. Show appreciation to yourself and others, by giving the gift of flowers.

Buy yourself flowers — This was just one of the amazing things I learned in the Tools to Life Program that changed my life (**www. toolstolife.com**)! When you take the time and resources, to buy yourself flowers, you are saying "I love me! I like me! I am worth it!" Flowers are beautiful and they will draw your eye and your nose to them as you enter a room, and they will be a constant reminder of the beauty that exists all around you. Flowers symbolize life, peacefulness and happiness, so be good to yourself and keep a small vase of flowers somewhere in your home. Please do not try to use money as an excuse not to buy yourself flowers. This is just part of your regular grocery shopping experience and as such, needs to be budgeted into your life. Grocery stores normally offer bouquets for under $10, so you don't need to make a second stop at the flower shop if you don't want to. If you have a few smaller vases, make one bouquet go the distance by putting 1 or 2 flowers in some small vases, and spread your vases strategically throughout your home. Place flowers on your bedside tables, in the bathroom, in the kitchen, on the mantle, and at the entryways. Flowers have a way of perking up any room. Dead flowers will suck positive energy, so be sure to change the water every day or two in your vases and compost or dispose of your flowers as soon as they start getting wilted.

Talk Nicely to Yourself — The way you talk to yourself can have a profound impact on how you feel about yourself. The same goes for your children. In this day and age, it is so easy to be hard on yourself, especially as a mom. Are you doing all you can for your kids? Are you providing them with every opportunity? Did you do that right? Could you have done something better? Think about how you talk to yourself, and consider the words you use when you actively talk to yourself in your head, or out loud.

No matter what you have done in the past, and no matter what your patterns of behavior have been in the past, it's time to put it all behind you and start loving yourself with your words. Treat each new day as a *Tabula Rasa*, a blank slate. Start fresh each day and only look forward in anticipation. Only say positive things to

Flowers-a little bouquet can go a long way! One bouquet of flowers can add flowers to several rooms in your home. This particular bouquet of daisy's cost me $8.99. I separated them and I was able to get 5 vases!

yourself. You totally believe everything you say to yourself, so if you say things like...

- "Things like this always happen to me"
- "I always do things wrong"
- "I can't do that"
- "There's no way I'll get that done"

You will believe what you say, and you will keep doing the very things that you don't want to do! We all make mistakes. The cool thing is that mistakes can be looked at as learning experiences, and as positive, enriching experiences. The minute we put a positive spin on a negative situation, we remove the negative power that the event may have been holding on us, and we are suddenly free to move forward. If you respect yourself, you will make an effort to talk to yourself like you are the most important person in the world, because you are. You have the power to change how you feel about yourself just by using positive words to fuel your inner spirit. It's time to start respecting YOU. Here are some amazing ways to talk to yourself:

- "That was incredible! You rocked the cookies for the soccer party! Go (insert your name here).
- "I did my very best and I sure learned a lot from that experience!"
- "I love my hair! I love my house! I love my kids! I love my car! I love my husband! I love my life!"
- "I can do ANYTHING if I put my mind to it!"

Give yourself credit where credit is due. You work hard for yourself and your family, and you should be proud of yourself for that! No one can make you feel as good about yourself as you can, so start giving yourself more pats on the back!

When the going gets tough, you're going to need a few techniques to keep you level. Here's my advice for keeping your girly cool.

"Calgon... take me away!"

Do you remember that TV commercial? A stressed-out mom in the midst of a hectic home full of screaming kids utters the phrase: "Calgon, take me away!" and, suddenly, is transported into a tranquil spa bathtub filled with bubbles and surrounded with candles. *Ahhhhh....*

Wouldn't it be great if it was just that easy? If you could think: "Calgon, Take Me Away!" and be magically transported to the place of your dreams? I'd like to say that it's not so farfetched. Hear me out.

When you are feeling upset or stressed or just a little off, try using your own mind to transport you to a place where you feel amazing: the spa, the bathtub, the beach, a hammock, a mountaintop, the golf course, under the sea, in your garden in the summertime when everything is in bloom... Close your eyes and really see yourself in that place. Take a couple of deep breaths and allow the feelings of being in that joyous place take over you. Even though you are not really there, your mind will immediately begin to relax and you will start to feel better. That is what we always want to focus on...feeling good all the time.

The "Calgon, Take Me Away" technique is useful in any situation and requires no props. Use it anytime you need a little getaway from the every day. If you really need a physical "Calgon getaway" here are a few easy ways to treat yourself right at home:

Meditate — Always remind yourself to breathe. There are still times when I find myself holding my breath. I'm not sure if this is just a holdover from my former smoking habit, or if it is just my innate reaction to stress. Whatever the reason, I can assure you that holding your breath is not good. When you are in pain, breathe through it. When you are frustrated, breathe through it. Take deeper and longer breaths whenever you can. It can be enlightening to focus on your breathing. We don't normally think about our breathing at all. It is an automatic bodily function that technically doesn't require any thought. But if you do focus on your breathing, you can use it to control your emotions and your body.

Take a minute to try this simple exercise:

> Find a quiet space and sit up tall. Roll your shoulders up and
> back and push them down (stick your chest out just a little); this
> will really increase the amount of space that your lungs have for
> breathing. Now close your eyes. Think only of your breathing and
> try to push away all other thoughts. Let any other thoughts that
> come into your head go, and focus on breathing through your nose.
> Breathe in through the nose for as long as you can, until your lungs
> feel nice and full. Pause for a second (hold your breath) before
> exhaling through your nose (no mouth breathing) as slowly as you
> can. Empty out your lungs as much as possible. Repeat this inhale-
> exhale cycle three times.

As you do these breathing exercises, focus on the space between the exhalation and inhalation. Think about that pause in your breath and the calm emptiness at that point. Focusing on something, like that little pause at the end or your inhale, will help to keep other thoughts at bay. Each time you repeat a breath, try to increase the amount of time that you take to inhale and exhale. Don't rush. You are increasing the amount of oxygen in your body, and decreasing the stress, emotion and worry. Each inhalation will add strength, vitality, and calm. Each exhalation will reduce stress and cleanse your body and mind. Welcome to the world of meditation!

This simple exercise shouldn't take more than two minutes, and can be done anywhere, at any time. It will help you focus on the day ahead. It can help calm you when your emotions are out of control. It can rejuvenate you when you are tired. Start with three breaths first thing in the morning and increase the amount of time you spend on this exercise when you feel ready. Try to get up to 15 minutes of meditation at the start of each day. Set a timer, and enjoy. It will help you relieve anxiety and deal with pain, frustration and disappointment. It will also ground you and help you tap into the power of the Universe so that you can create things in your life more easily. The more you meditate, the more you will think consciously about your breath, which will encourage you to take deeper, more cleansing breaths. Everyone has time for this easy exercise that can change your life — for the better.

Give yourself the gift of time — As mom's, our inner girl may get a little lost in the family shuffle. Everyone in the family has stuff going on and we can't do it all for everyone. You are important, and your inner girl deserves to have a little time of her own during the week. You deserve to reward all the hard work that you do for your family with some time for you. Each week, you should be scheduling in some time to focus on activities that you want to do. Get out once a week for a fitness class, coffee with a friend, a sporting event, the theatre, a movie, and make this event about you. Plan a date with your partner and get a babysitter, or go out on your own while your partner stays home with the kids. Life gets so busy and hectic with your family that it can make you feel guilty at times to want to do "your own thing". But you are worth it! You deserve it! All you need to do is schedule that time in, and the rest will magically fall into place. Do it. You're worth it! In addition to your once per week outing, give yourself 15 minutes of time each day, or longer once you get comfortable with it. Slow down and relax, just for 15. You may choose to meditate, read, take a walk, or just sit quietly with a tea or coffee. That's 15 minutes all at one time, ladies. You have to take it all at once!

Spirituality-Love of the Universe — Tapping into the amazing loving energy that is flowing all around us is my idea of spirituality, and I like to call it the Universe. No matter what you call it, believing in something without being able to see it is true faith. I may not be able to see it, but I know that I can feel the energy. You will feel it too when you start meditating. That tingly energy coursing through your fingertips and all across your body is the Universe.

I believe it is important to be thankful for everything that we have in our lives, and I believe we have the Universe to thank. Take time in your day to just look up and around and say "thank you" for anything that comes to mind…your health, the trees, yourself, the ocean, anything and everything. Sending out thankfulness energy is extremely positive and a great way of sharing energy. You get what you give, so that great energy will also multiply back to you.

The Universe is giving and loving. It wants to provide you with anything your heart may desire. Ask, and you shall receive. If you believe something to be true, then it is true. Start using it to your advantage and ask for some really cool stuff!

You really can do anything if you put your mind to it, because the Universe will always have your back. The Universe works in mysterious ways, and if you are observant and you have a little faith, you will begin to see miracles happening around you every day. One of my favorite ways the Universe shows me it is there is through those crazy, little coincidences that we experience in our lives. I believe there is no such thing as a coincidence…you and the Universe create it!

All of these flyers arrived at once about a week after Ryan and I were discussing needing all of this information. Ask, and it is given!

Recently, my husband Ryan was talking about resealing our cracking driveway, getting a delivery of mulch and dirt for the garden, and also getting a new pair of glasses. A few days later, I got the mail and the 3 flyers included with our regular post was for "The Bark Mulch Depot, "Bow River Paving", and "Lenscrafters". I am not kidding.

Ryan and I were both like, "that is too weird". But it's not actually that weird. Ryan was focusing on those things by thinking about them, so he drew that energy to him. Strange coincidence, or energy? Start watching your own life for these little miracles. They will start seeming less odd each time it happens. Your confidence in yourself and the Universe will get stronger and you will be able to create things more easily.

When you are focused on a goal, try to go with the flow and let things happen naturally. You may hit roadblocks along the way, or be taken off a path that you thought you'd stay on forever, and it is important in these moments to maintain your focus on the prize. Things are not always going to happen the way you thought they might, and that is ok. Things will happen exactly as they are supposed to, if you allow them to. You confidence in the Universe may wane when things don't go the way you thought they might. What is interesting is you will get there no matter what, if you remain positive and stay focused. The path you have laid out in your head is not the only path, and you must remain open to traveling down new pathways. Do not give up when things get hard! Enjoy every minute of the journey and just let it be!

Watch for opportunities — You must have your eyes and ears open and be actively looking for opportunities. The Universe can give you what you need, but you have to be willing to put some effort into finding the opportunity. James Redfield's book 'The Celestine Prophecy', really gave me some insight into coincidences and opportunities.

Bottom line — Ask a lot of questions when you meet new people...why are you meeting them? What kind of information do they have for you, or do you have for them? Why is certain information being presented to you in the form of a book, email, a letter etc. Look for opportunity in everything that is put in front of you. You will be amazed at what you start learning.

The Invisible Shield —You can also use your mind and the Universe to protect yourself, and your family. I like to call it using your 'invisible shield'. I think about, and focus on, a huge shield that is all protecting. I project this shield around myself, my children, my husband and our home at all times. It makes me feel protected and safe, and if I believe I am protected and safe, I will be. I will continue to bring that positive life giving energy into my circle. The invisible shield concept works extremely well with children, especially if you start it early on. Kids tend to develop fears and insecurities as they grow. Tell them to always keep their invisible shields on all day and while they are sleeping. If they feel afraid, or scared, tell them to think about their invisible shield surrounding them with warmth and security and strength. Ask them if they can feel the energy of the shield around them. Help them learn how to project their own shields. Your children will feel more secure knowing that they are always protected by the shield, and it is a coping strategy that they can use throughout their lives that may actually work to keep them safe. It's worth a shot.

Nothing can penetrate that invisible shield. Believe it and use it. Calm yourself and protect yourself. Once you have your shield on (and that should be all the time), you can stop thinking about all of the bad things that might happen to you, because they won't. Once you stop thinking about those negative things, you will be even more protected against them. It will be easier for you to think about awesome things, and you will attract more awesomeness into your life.

Make conscious choices about what you think about. Give yourself time, lots of it. Prioritize and only do things that feel good to you. Have fun, have a blast, create your destiny right now. You are who you are because you define yourself that way. Redefine yourself if you want and embrace YOU.

You have started to unleash your inner girl, and by now she is pretty excited to be back in the driver's seat! You are 'That Girl', Mommy! Once you start treating yourself as the gorgeous, amazing woman that you are, you will really start to embrace yourself as you are, and your confidence is going to soar! You are learning to treat yourself as you deserve to be treated. *What else could a girl want?* It's time to add a little love to your life.

CHAPTER 12
All You Need Is Love

* *

"Love is something, if you give it away, you'll end up having more!"
– Popular Children's Bible Song

Love is all YOU need. Can that really be true? Can one live on love alone? As people, we have survived and thrived under truly grueling circumstances, and we always prevail. Perhaps we can't live on love alone, but I do feel that we NEED love. Our minds need love and our bodies need love. Love feels good. Feeling good is the ultimate prize, so love must surely be something that we need.

Love can be expressed in so many different ways: a kind word, a gentle touch, a hug, a kiss, or a loving slap on the ass. People need all kinds of love. When you are shown love, it is easy to pass it on, or pay it forward. Positive attracts positive and love attracts love. Love inspires you to help, to be generous, to be patient, to be kind, and to be forgiving. Love makes you smile. Seeing a mom cuddling her new baby, or a dad with his sweet daughters' hand in his as they stroll through the mall, will bring joy to your heart. That is love.

As mom's, we are all absolutely incredible at loving others. Our magic kisses heal boo boos, our Kleenex dries their crying eyes, and our arms hug them when their feelings are so hurt that there

is nothing else to do but sob. As mom's we are strong and passionate with our children, and with our partners. We know when we are needed, and we make sure we are there! We joyously celebrate every victory and we make the little bumps in the road softer. We love our children and would do anything for them. We are all amazing moms. In fact, we are "Those Moms", and thank goodness! We are responsible for creating a new generation. We will go on in our children, in our Grandchildren, and in our Great-Grandchildren, whether we like it or not! That is a given.

It's time for you, Mom, to start getting the love you deserve everyday! When you turn your focus back onto yourself, you will

realize that by helping yourself to be happy, by loving yourself, and collecting love from others, you will actually teach others around you about love. You will create a path of love and happiness for the people in your life to follow. In helping yourself, you will have no choice but to help others. And getting that love is going to feel really good…in all the right places!

Here are a few fantastic ways to "share the love":

4 Hugs a Day

Through our many years of preschool, our family learned a very valuable little song, "4 Hugs a Day", which clearly states that "4 hugs a day is the MINIMUM…not the maximum" number of hugs that we need in one day! Do yourself a favor and make sure you get at least 4 hugs every day. Hugging creates amazing positive energy. It allows you to share your amazingness with others, and have others share their amazingness with you. Strive to get 4 hugs a day, and try to make each one nice and long. I just love to hug people, and I am often told by people that I have the best hugs. You know what my secret is? When I hug, I am not afraid; I am very much aware and present. I love to grab the person that I am hugging and create that amazing feeling of togetherness, because in reality, we are one. The longer you hold a hug for, the more energy is created. So hold it for as long as you can, without being totally creepy. When you hug someone, it should make you feel warm and safe. As a society, I believe we are lacking in the "touch" department, for a lot of different reasons. You don't have to go hugging a whole bunch of different people throughout the day; that is not what this is about. Be selective with who you give hugs to, and perhaps increase the frequency and duration of hugging that you do with the people close to you. 4 hugs a day is the minimum…get out your journal and start keeping track of your hugs. Get 4, add more, and let's see what happens!

Touch Yourself-Love Yourself

While we long to be loved by others, it is in loving ourselves that we can really find ourselves, and help others love us better. As women, we need to feel free to touch our own bodies to satisfy our "needs", as well as just make ourselves feel good. When we feel comfortable enough to love our own bodies, we become aware of our bodies on a totally different level. What feels good, and what doesn't. Fast or slow, soft or hard, you need to learn what your preferences are so that you can communicate your preferences to others.

Loving yourself and touching yourself is a great thing. And... it's something that no one else needs to know about. It is your private relationship with yourself that you can nurture throughout your life. When it comes to touching yourself, it doesn't just have to be about masturbation.

Recently, I visited a spa and while I was getting my facial, I became acutely aware of how gently and lovingly the esthetician was wiping my face with the warm cloth. It made me realize how carelessly I was treating my own body when I was washing my face, or scrubbing my body! Just slip, slosh, slap...no time for pampering! Our bodies are our temples, and again, the way we treat our own bodies can reflect how we feel about ourselves. When you are putting cream on your body, or washing your body, rub yourself lovingly and gently. You deserve to be pampered by YOU! I recently tested a Teabag Bath. I love tea and a friend of mine gave me some bath teabags. The bath tea looks exactly like an oversized teabag, stuffed with delicious smelling herbs. One night, I ran my bath and dropped one in. It smelled delicious. I got in the bath, put my head back, and then put the tea bag on my eyes as an eye bag. *Ahhhhh*.... When I'd had enough of that, I soaked the tea bag back in the water and proceeded to use it like a sponge over my entire body. It was a glorious bath, relaxing, and invigorating, something a little new! Just giving myself that time out to enjoy a bath made me appreciate myself more. I am worth a teabag bath!

When it comes to touching yourself intimately, there is only one rule…If it feels good, I want you to do it, and do lots of it. You should be very comfortable touching yourself lovingly. Explore your own body with your fingers, and feel free to use props and tools if they are available. If you have no experience with props in this department, but you are curious, go to an adult store one night during the week. The staff are very knowledgeable and at ease with these subjects and they can easily recommend something for you to start with. Instead of feeling ashamed about touching your body, you should feel excited. IT IS YOUR BODY. You will never have to rely on someone to please you when you can do it for yourself. Instead, you can look for someone to enhance your experiences. If you have never ventured into this kind of thing before, you may want to start with a nice warm shower, or bath, and wash your body lovingly.

Turn your thoughts to sex, and think about how good it feels to be touched and loved. Think about your partner, or your fantasy partner. Use your imagination to start your internal fire, and then use your fingers to stoke the fire. If you simply cannot imagine anything sexual in your own head, there are videos you can watch that will get you in the mood. Speak to your adult store staff member for more details. Having a good sexual relationship with yourself will translate into having a good sexual relationship with a partner. If you just want to have sex a couple of times to make babies and you're not into having any fun with sex, then don't bother trying. But if you want to maintain a healthy love relationship with yourself and your partner now, and for years and years to come, you must think of sex as a whole new relationship. You need to know what you like, what you don't like, and you need to be able to communicate that to your partner through actions or words. Be kind to yourself with your touch no matter what part of the body you are touching. You have the power to make yourself feel good in every way!

Getting the LOVE.

Making love, having sex, doing the deed, no matter what you call it, having sex is an animal instinct that ensures that we are not the final generation! Humans are sexual beings, and our bodies were designed to make sex pleasurable so that we would do it and keep the cycle of life going. Having sex should be fun. It is a form of exercise, and it can make you feel happier and live longer (according to a recent article I read by Dr. Oz!).

I think we all want to be happier and live longer. Is sex the answer? I don't know, but if it feels good, do it!

Being touched intimately by someone else is a treat, and it can take you to places you may never have been before! It can make you feel incredible, relaxed, and revitalized. But only if you are in the mood for it, right ladies!

As mom's, our time is valuable. We always have a million things on the go and our minds may be racing with schedules, grocery lists, and to do lists. By the time the kids are in bed at night, you may feel like a freight train has run you over and you are flatter than a pancake on your bed. If that's the case, you need to slow down a little! Making love, and being "turned on" sexually is a mind game, which explains why men are more easily able to get in the game at short notice...they think about sex several times throughout the day! Mom's don't have time to think about sex! Do we?

Yes, you do have time. If you want to increase the action between the sheets, you need to be getting your head in the game throughout the day. You started with your lingerie, and now you are sexy and smooth. Throughout the day, take 30 seconds to think about something sexual...perhaps a favorite move that your partner does, or maybe a thought about your fantasy man and what he might do for you, or just think about how good it feels to touch your own (insert favorite place here). You may feel a little silly about this at first, but over time, it will be easier for you to think pleasantly about sex. The more positive you are about your thoughts, the more exciting you will make this for yourself and your partner. Try to think about sex 3 times throughout the day. If you find it difficult to think about sex, I would suggest sitting down with a good book to help get you in the mood. Juicy books, like "50 Shades of Grey", or the "Lover" series by J.R. Ward, are packed with great ideas and content to get even a novice going.

See how you feel at the end of the day. You may hug your partner a little longer when they come home, and perhaps you'll whisper something in their ear about meeting in the bedroom later!

No matter how tired you are, you will have anticipation on your side. When you are focused on something, you will find the time and the energy to get into it. Don't bother turning the TV on once the kids are in bed. Instead, turn the lights on low in your room, strip down to your lingerie, put on your heels and call your mate into your lair. Take as much time as you need and be sure to thoroughly enjoy every minute. Allow someone else to pay attention to your body in all the right ways. Sometimes it's quick and hard, and sometimes it is long and slow - enjoy it! It is supposed to feel good.

Do not be afraid to offer encouragement to your partner when something feels good (oh yes, keep doing that, uh huh, right there, etc.), and also loving nudges in the right direction when they may be off track (faster, slower, to the right, go back to where you were, not there...here (help them get in the right places). Your partner will be thrilled to pleasure you properly and you will be getting it where you want it. Talking dirty in the bedroom can make things super steamy!

Here is another great way to get in the mood for love:

Italian Getaway Bath or Picnic

This is the kind of bath that you want to share with someone special. First, you will need to prepare your nosh. Get out a platter, or a few baskets and cut up a baguette, some soft mozza cheese (or your favorite), and then add some olives, and chocolate. Open up a nice bottle of Chianti, and bring two glasses. Figure out a way to have the food and drinks accessible while you sit in the bathtub, together. You may need to bring in a small table to put beside the tub. Draw the drapes and run a bath for 2. Sprinkle in flower petals (if you have them), or some delicious smelling bath salts. Light some candles around the tub and get your towels out. If this simply will not work in the bath, add a picnic style blanket to your bed and do it there. Invite your partner to share in a relaxing theme inspired bath or picnic. I used Italy for this example as it reminds me of the trip Ryan and I took for our 10 year anniversary, without any kids for 2 and a half weeks. Use any theme that you like, and keep it simple so you can do it often.

Make the time you spend together as a couple fun and exciting. Planning special little surprises like this one will show your partner how much you care about them, and about your relationship. Ladies, this is also an easy one for your men to plan once they know how rewarding it is. Friday nights at home are going to get more exciting.

You deserve to enjoy great sex, so be good to yourself and get the party started. You can bet your partner will be pleased.

"If it feels good, do it!" is a rule you can use to judge everything that you do in your life. Life is supposed to feel good, so always make good choices for YOU!

Epilogue

I hope that you have enjoyed your Mom Makeover and that you are seeing the visible effects of that makeover in every area of your life. I also hope that you have enjoyed reading this book... though I'm guessing that you did a lot more than just read it. The ideas and advice I am passing on to you will stick with you and help you whenever you need them.

If you are already feeling the urge to make a change, just go for it! You're ready to implement the techniques. If you don't yet feel the urge to throw caution to the wind, and clean out your fridge or your closet, or get your kids working for you, don't worry. **Be That Mom** will still be here waiting for you when you are ready. The information you need has already been safely planted in your mind, so when you are ready, you will know what to do.

The world needs moms. Loving, kind, caring, patient, happy, smiling, amazing, gorgeous, healthy, organized, successful, joyful moms! As a mom, you have the ability to show your children how to embrace themselves and others with love, and to teach them how to care for themselves in loving ways. Mom's are incredible role models who have little people watching carefully over what they do. When we treat ourselves with care, attention and love, our children will do the same, and so on, and so on, and so on. Mom's can change the world in so many ways.

No matter what age your kids are, be sure to take some time right away to hug them, kiss them and tell them that you love them. Tell them how much you care about them, and appreciate all the things they do for you, and for your family. Then, I want you to do the same to yourself.

I am incredibly excited for you! Together we have discovered what your priorities are, where your clutter is, and what's in your lingerie drawer (or not in there). I hope you are excited to get your energy and your life moving in the right direction, and I trust that you are going to pay yourself the attention you deserve.

Don't forget to pay attention to your home and your schedule too. Doing little things consistently is what makes all the difference in your efficiency, organization and time management. When you have control of your external surroundings, it is reflected internally. You will be on time, calm, focused, and relaxed. So do a little maintenance every day!

Remember, you may be able to live on love alone, so nurture the love relationships in your life, and don't worry so much about "things". Enjoy every moment and smile more often on purpose.

Now get out there and conquer the world, Mom. And make sure you keep in touch.

Tina

Acknowledgements

"The way a team plays as a whole determines its success.
You may have the greatest bunch of individual stars in the world,
but if they don't play together, the club won't be worth a dime."
-Babe Ruth

What does it take to write a book? For me, it has taken years of thinking, months of writing, hours of babysitting, tons of support and a lot of laughter. A project like this takes more than just "That Girl", it takes a family, an editor or two, a business manager, a graphic designer, a cousin or two, more family, a book designer, a photographer, some mentors, a publisher... my list could go on.

For now, I'd like to take this opportunity to recognize some amazing people who have been with me through this incredible journey. Thanks for helping me secure 'The Summer to Remember' this year with my kids...my first summer off (as soon as I can get this book done!).

My Husband Ryan. It's not always easy to run a busy household filled with independent girls, but if anyone can do it, Ryan, you are the one. You consistently support and encourage my crazy adventures, and you are always willing to go the extra mile (lemonade stand superman!). Thank you for helping me "find" time to write this book, and for always being ready for anything. You are "That Guy"! XOXOXOXOXO

My girls, Trinity, Kayley and Payton. Now you are 9, 7 and 5 years old... Wow, how time flies! Right now, you have all found it very irritating that I am writing this book! I frequently hear "Mom! You are always on your computer!" "You never play with us!" "Why do you have to do that book?" Well, one day you will read my book and see all the wonderful pictures of the things we HAVE done together, and I hope you will agree that it was totally worth every minute. Plus, those pictures prove that I do play with you...ha ha! You are three of the most amazing little girls and I cannot wait to see what you will do in life!

Janet (aka Mom/Grandma) and Don (Pepere). Words cannot express my gratitude to both of you for everything you do for me! Hours of babysitting, hours of website maintenance, hours of video editing, and hours of Wednesdays! I am totally and utterly grateful to both of you for the support you have shown me right from the start. Mom— your belief in me and your faith in me has been unwavering. You are totally "That Mom", and I love you to bits!

Charlene (aka Nana). I was only 15 when Ryan brought me home to meet you, and I don't really know if you were all that thrilled! Thanks for being a constant source of strength in my life. You were like a mom to me from the start. I have always looked up to the relationship that you and Terry have, and the type of Mother, and Nana that you are. You and Terry can still light up the dance floor with your flashy jive moves...something Ryan and I aspire to do! Thank you for all that you have done for me over the years! You have logged a lot of babysitting hours, baked a ton of cookies and helped outfit the girls in all the latest Value Village finds. You are an incredible shopper, and I love your "Do-it-Now" mentality when it comes to thrift store projects. You are "That Nana!"

Cindy Lou Who. Now you are a girl after my own heart. With 4 kids and a passion for soccer, I could not have a more competent, Kick Butt, Get-er-done kind of "Mom "Manager than you.

You have made miracles happen, you never drop the ball, and you always look amazing! Not too many people can keep me in line… but you come pretty close, and that's sayin' something!

Shelley Arnusch. We have really come a long way together, baby. And we're not done yet! You have pulled material out of me that I didn't even know existed…but you knew it was there when no one else would have. You have been an integral piece of the Be That Books team from the start, and I am looking forward to seeing your children's book, *Too Many Teddies*, on the shelves of bookstores everywhere!

Samantha. (aka Sami). At just the time when I needed you, you appeared. Oddly enough, you were brought to me through your beautiful daughter, Avery, who has become lovely friends with my daughter. Coincidence? I think not! You are not afraid of a little commitment and a lot of hard work! Talk about pushing some serious deadlines…but for you, Mom, no problem. Here's to the first of many books together!

My cousin, Julie. How does one thank someone who drops everything in their lives to tour the world with me? You have made every book signing, TV appearance and hotel stay more exciting and hilarious. The more time I get to spend with you, the more I want! Thanks for always knowing what I need — you and I are quite the duo!

Teamwork is the only way to really get stuff done efficiently. I am so thankful for all the people that are on my teams!

People will come, and people will go, but remember that every person that comes into your life adds something to it. So, I will leave with you a thought, and a song. Never burn your bridges, and always keep your eyes open for new opportunity.

"Make new friends, but keep the old. One is Silver and the other gold". — Popular Farewell Song

May you have lots of silver and gold in your life from here on out.

Tina and her family live in Calgary, Alberta, Canada.

www.bethatmomnow.com

www.bethatmomnow.com

Proudly Published by
Be That Books™

Books on Motivation.
Books on Organization.
Books on Change.

www.bethatbooks.com

Check out our other books.

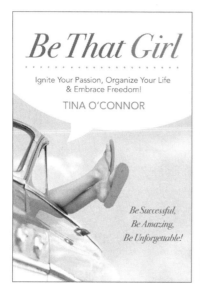

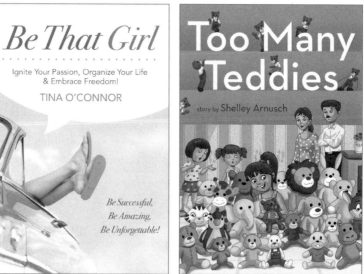